AF608560

CINDY SHERMAN

CLOWNS

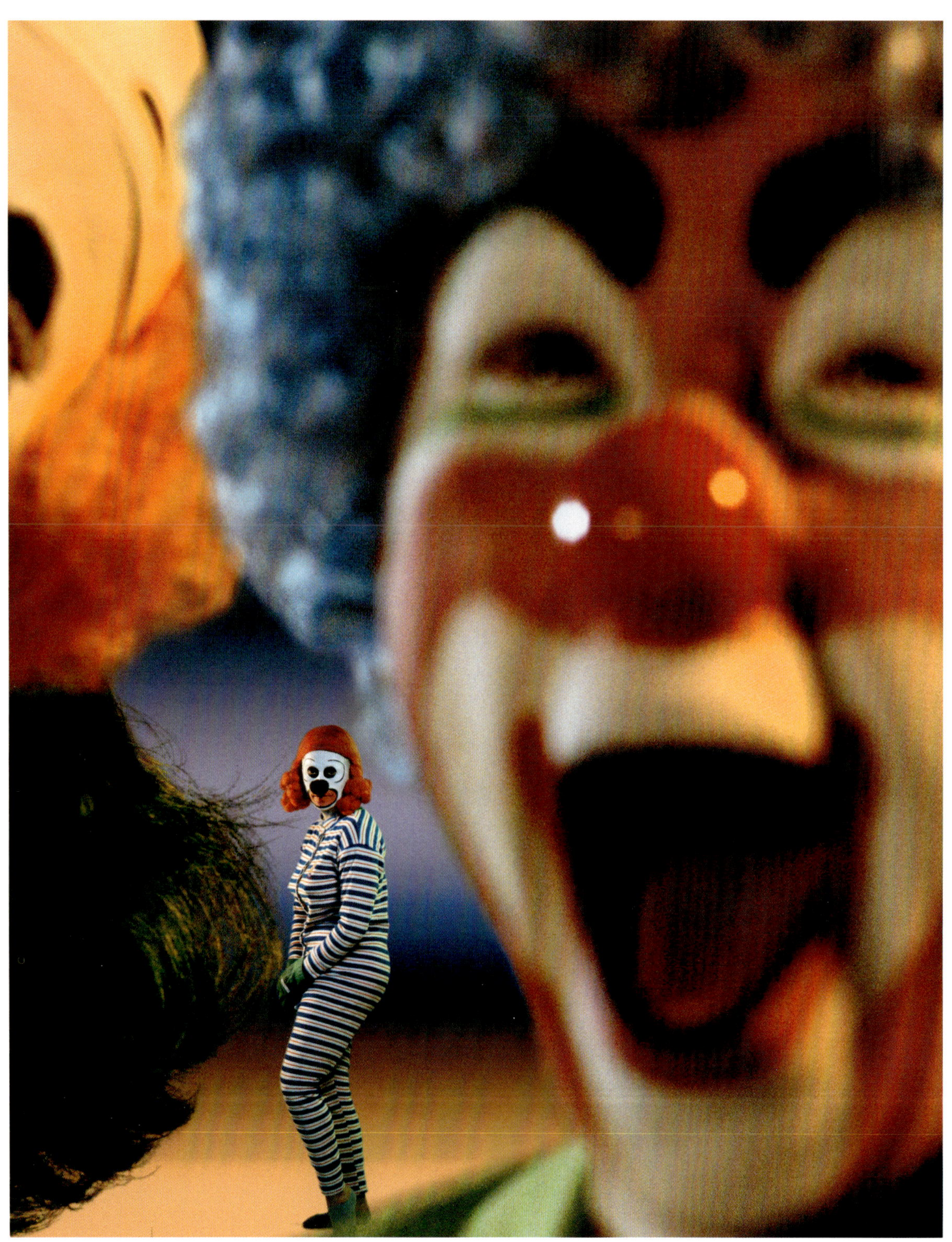

CINDY SHERMAN
CLOWNS

Text von | Essay by

MAIK SCHLÜTER

Interview

CINDY SHERMAN & ISABELLE GRAW

SCHIRMER/MOSEL

in Zusammenarbeit mit | in cooperation with

kestnergesellschaft, Hannover

PREFACE

Without a doubt, Cindy Sherman is one of the truly great and important artists of our day. Ever since her early work, the *Untitled Film Stills* made in 1977–80, she has focused on questions of identity and changed roles. In her series of photographs Cindy Sherman has always assumed a dual role, namely that of artist and actress. Indeed, even in her latest series, she has been busy hiding herself behind the many-faceted masquerade of a clown. And by using digital image processing technology she is able to multiply herself and stage herself as a group of persons. Precisely the vibrant colors of the likewise digitally created backgrounds lend this garish travesty even greater intensity. With her work, Cindy Sherman manages repeatedly to find new contemporary forms of representation and to consistently advance the topics and subjects she addresses. The series published here is a further impressive example of her creativity as an artist.

We are very proud to be the first institution in Europe to present Cindy Sherman's new works and to be able to accompany them with a monograph. I am deeply grateful to Cindy Sherman for the trust she has had in us and for honoring the kestnergesellschaft by giving us the opportunity to premiere this new series of works. A not inconsiderable part was played here by the gallery owner who has for many years represented the artist, Monika Sprüth, for she acted as the intermediary who enabled the exhibition to come about in the first place. I would like to thank her and her staff most cordially for their ever professional and marvelous support. My thanks also go to Janelle Reiring and Helene Winer at Metro Pictures, the artist's New York gallery, for the part they played in ensuring the show was a success.

We have been very fortunate to have been able to publish the catalog with Lothar Schirmer, a well-known expert on the œuvre of Cindy Sherman who has already published a number of outstanding volumes on her work. I would especially like to thank Isabelle Graw for conducting an interview with Cindy Sherman in New York – it offers a personal glimpse into how the artist works. And last but not least I would like to thank Maik Schlüter, the curator of the show, for his careful preparatory work for the exhibition and the catalog, his insightful essay and the perfect presentation of the works in our halls.

Veit Görner, Director of the kestnergesellschaft

FUN THAT IS NO FUN

Maik Schlüter

As a figure, the clown is considered the agent of unbridled enjoyment, an open-minded fun-merchant who captivates everyone, especially the kids. He is a fool who gets walloped instead of the audience, and stumbles from one misfortune to the next, always under the schadenfreude-filled eyes of those who are themselves actually the victims of the shallowness and injustice of life. Clowns are a screen onto which the enjoyment of the suffering of others can be projected. This suffering is staged either as a melancholic gesture, as enigmatic irony or as brash slapstick. The spectrum of his activities ranges from depicting the serious and sad loser via the silent and wondrous magician through to the loud anarchist, who turns all the rules upside down. All these characters have something contradictory about them, for while stimulating the positive sides to our emotions, prompting laughter and amazement, they likewise reference the limits and repression of normalcy, not to mention the world's incomplete and unpredictable character. The act of fun is forever orbiting the tragedy of life. The clown has something impenetrable about him, for he displays a huge and obscene smile, pointing up each of his actions. You never really know in what trap set by the netherworld he will be ensnared and who will be the next victim of his jokes. Precisely the contradiction between his joyous grimace and the cunning and fickle nature of his actions is what makes this shimmering figure so appealing. After all, behind the colorful mask lurks death, which brutally, ineluctably and consistently rules over the world and humans so unexpectedly. Truth is ambiguous in this regard: the vivaciousness of laughter is the power to overcome fear and loss, while also manifesting the impotent attempt to counter the irreversible. But even on a smaller scale, the clown offers enlightenment, showing the audience (as the court jester once did the king) a diluted version of its own inadequacies and errors. But like the ruler, the remainder of society can only tolerate itself in the mirror held up to it by the picaresque entertainment. The focus here is channeling, not change, not enlightening insight into the status quo, only on weakening and softening the impact of the latter. The goal: to make the conditions and inner constellations more tolerable.

In Cindy Sherman's new work dating from 2003-4 the clown takes the stage as a strident transfer of a gaiety as fake as it is false. Each smile, each theatrical gesture is either permeated by abysmal maliciousness, by helpless solitude, by idiotic simpleness or by superficial sexualization. In this new work, Sherman pursues the interests formulated in her earlier works: social role allocations, highlighting repressed joys, fears and violence and forever addressing the question as to the adequate images of social reality. Sherman does not present the sad Pierrot. Nor does she show the skeptic or melancholic who is aware of all the failure in the worlds and yet, or precisely despite this, tries to entertain his audience, and then hides his own tears. Instead, we see the exaggerated and commercial variant of the clown.

Strident and aggressive make-up transforms the individual into an eccentric product of permanent and above all irritating gaiety. He or she is a market crier like Ronald McDonald who entrances the kids and blackmails the parents: "Surely you hardly want to drag your children away from our birthday party simply because our fast-food and cheap toys cost a handful of dollars more?"

That said, clowns can do more; they are not only multipliers and eye-catchers for advertising, but also a fixed part of circus culture. However, we know just how unromantic the romantic image of the touring troupe of artistes actually is. The reality is less free love and poetic inspiration and more hard graft, meager pay and little recognition. In the case of the clown, this means being professionally funny, spontaneous and yet controlled in showing the people what they want to see: themselves and yet someone else. Yet the game with the role of substitute is dangerous, as it is shot through with a fundamental dishonesty. It is not the whole person that is on display, but only his risible and contour-free copy. The heights and the depths remain concealed, the edge to the full scope and tragedy of human action is blunted. This means for the clown and his repertoire that the rubber truncheon is actually a guillotine or machine gun, the chair pulled out suddenly and the funny irritant correspond to torture and each instance of lying on the ground is tantamount to a sexual attack, an act of violence. Admittedly, the clown's superficial tenderness is also an expression of possible sympathy and love. But Cindy Sherman's clowns do not speak of this. Malicious and contorted are their masks, and Sherman shows us clowns who are lustful and sadistic, mean and impenetrable, brutal and deceiving. And she puts it all in a world full of tricks and contradictions, with laughter that gets stuck in your throat. These are images that invariably impact us and show how stupid and naïve the wish for "clownish" entertainment is. The contradiction evident in the sad Pierrot is lent harsher form in Sherman's work and taken to the extreme.

In this context, Sherman's clowns can be compared with other works of contemporary art, such as Bruce Nauman's *Clown Torture* (1987), an oppressive installation which shows the constantly identical, vacuous and helpless gestures and words of the brash fun-merchant and leaves it open as to who is torturing whom; Paul McCarthy's *Painter* (1995), who presents the painter as a witless joke figure, who by pure chance achieves respectable and creative results and on top of which is hardly taken seriously by the audience; Jonathan Borofsky's *The Dancing Clown at 2,845,325* (1982-3), an uncanny and monstrous hybrid of ballerina and clown, at once graceful and tragic, sad and ridiculous; or Ugo Rondinone's collapsed and fat clowns (*If There Were Anywhere But Desert: Tuesday*, 2002), who sit or lie exhausted on the ground – sad variety players, burned out by the constant tightrope walk between good cheer and inner abyss, between slavering and applause.

All of these works show not the clown as artist, but the artist as clown, and refuse to afford any positive identification with them as sensitive outsiders or jesting enlighteners. In the McCarthy piece, the painter squeezes the paint onto his pallet from an out-sized tube labeled "SHIT" and then starts completely smearing over the canvas in his somehow strangely isolated studio. That is the praxis of high art and its reception: fictitious abilities and values are created, art is nothing more than the result of speculation, and the artist a compliant idiot who is stuck at the anal retentive phase. If the show and above all the stereotypes of the irresponsible and unreflective artist are true, then everything can be sold and the audience has art where it wants it, on the verges of society, as anarchic and at best decorative entertainment. We can see something similar in the work of Nauman, Borofsky, Rondione or Sherman. The figure of the artist is never taken completely seriously, it has to play a defined and constrained role, the tragicomic hero who concerns himself or herself with curiosities and splenetic ideas, the results of which are not readily comprehensible because art from the outset is not construed as a central variable in social life but always only as the expression of entertaining, contemplative or irrational luxury that, as most, goes hand in hand with abysmal and suppressed feelings. And it is here that our expectations as regards clowns and as regards artists overlap: they have to be representatives for the implicit emotional life of the audience, something the audience never lives. The clown/artist is a figure whose statements and actions are always perceived beneath the lacquer of artistic mystification and that are thus sufficiently removed from our personal lives to be legible as real criticism.

At this point Cindy Sherman contradicts things and gives the audience what it deserves: the viewers are confronted with themselves as idiots and malicious m-o-c's who can never hope to be calmed or distracted by art. Sherman chooses the game of masquerade to this end. And why not read this game as a very direct metaphor of social life, as a strategy of disquieting, as a false-friendly image that wishes to deceive us as to the real base intentions in social coexistence? Or to put it in less general terms, as a sexualized and violent mask that veils or replaces identity for the moment of so-called perversion and enables the person behind it to fuck, beat, torture or deploy more subtle forms of mastery and repression in the name of someone else? The mask here is an expression of the schizoid ambiguity and contradictory nature that is lived out every day: the clown becomes the symbol of alienation. And Cindy Sherman uses the mimic repertoire of the inscrutable and intensified to still further the audience's fantasies of fear and joy. Even if the show has to go on, at the end of the day everyone laughs about the fact that there is nothing to laugh about.

NO MAKE-UP

An Interview with Cindy Sherman, by Isabelle Graw

Graw: I wanted to suggest that we talk about your artistic procedure, and I don't mean that I'm interested in tracing out your authentic work process, but the procedure *implied* in your work. It seems to me as if there's an experimental protocol set up for each series. But in setting these parameters, chance and the arbitrary also play a role. I'm interested in the extent to which you seek out and provoke these contingencies. Take your early work *Bus Riders* (1976/2000) with its repeated set up: a chair, a visible cable, and a certain spatial situation. What happens here has a certain dynamic all its own—different types are played out. You take them on, form them, but also give yourself over to them.

Sherman: When you say, "give yourself over," do you mean a form of self-sacrifice?

Graw: Yes, self-sacrifice as an artistic method. Basically, that's an old modernist issue. But modernist critics like Clement Greenberg assumed that the material provides certain guidelines that the artist has to fulfill, as if these guidelines where a given. I would formulate it less normatively and as a necessity of production aesthetics, that artists as a rule subject themselves to certain guidelines which they themselves have chosen. The clowns theme of your new works, for example, is totally overdetermined in art historical terms. I must admit that I usually have an acute aversion to clowns and everything they suggest—the mask or cliché of the "sad clown."

Sherman: I think all people feel that, especially in this country [the United States].

Graw: How so?

Sherman: I met a clown who studied in Paris at a famous clown school who told me that this clown phobia is particularly notable in America because of the many clowns used here in advertising, children's television shows, and the like, and that these clowns have become more and more horrible and terrifying. Clowns aren't seen here as an art form, something that's different in Europe.

Graw: From Picasso paintings to Fellini films, the clown serves as a surface for artistic projections. When I had a look at your clown pictures, however, I asked myself whether clowns were actually at issue. Are there clowns that paint teeth onto their mouths in such a grotesque, monstrous fashion? It seemed you only used the given guidelines "clowns" in order to explode its conventions and go much further.

Sherman: Yes. I didn't want to just do traditional portraits of clowns, but push things further. But there actually are clowns with teeth painted on their mouths. As a guide I started with depictions of clowns that I found in books or on the Internet. The greatest challenge for me was to allow a personality to emerge from behind the clown make-up: a personality that has nothing to do with my own. It was important to me that each one of these personalities looks different: I wanted in a way to find something behind the make-up, something that shimmers through.

Graw: The format "clowns" also allows you to keep from showing even a centimeter of naked flesh. There are only a few places where your neck—also covered in make up—is visible. But otherwise your body is completely covered, and you're wearing wigs, broad collars, long, oversized felt gloves, giving the image's surface the texture of a fabric painting.

Sherman: There are, however, a few early clown pictures where you can still see my hands. I covered them with make-up until I read somewhere that clowns always wear gloves.

Graw: Even though it's you taking on the role of depicting the clowns, you show nothing and expose nothing of yourself. This trend towards withdrawal was present in earlier works as well, but it seemed to me as if you were pushing it to a new extreme in this work.

Sherman: No, that had more to do with the clown tradition itself. Even in the earlier works, as in the portraits of women I made in the year 2000, I always used make-up when my arms or other skin layers were visible. I wanted to complement the make-up in my face, letting everything appear seamless. The skin of my arms was supposed to be identical with that of my face.

Graw: So my impression that the clown subject has something to do with the desire to make yourself completely invisible is wrong?

Sherman: I didn't think about it that way. What attracted me to clowns was instead the possibility of stepping into different clown personalities that allowed me multiple layers of meaning: the potential of being sad, disturbed, a psycho killer. I'm interested in what I imagine about the person who's made up as a clown. What makes this person to want to be a clown? It's probably usually the genuine pleasure in making people laugh. But I was more interested in those clown types where it seemed there was something skewed in their personality, something disturbed.

Graw: The gaze of these clowns is always clouded and empty. Dull, expressionless eyes that seem to look nowhere. Their gaze no longer has an addressee. Even in the pictures with a number of clown figures, no relationship to the beholder is being sought out.

Sherman: That might be due to the structure of the pictures: I was thinking of circus posters. These pictures are supposed to look as if they were simply cut out of an advertisement for the circus, with a stiff and artificial pose to sell the idea of the funny clown although my clowns are anything but funny.

Graw: The digitally produced backgrounds in neon colors look like psychedelic wallpaper or Op Art patterns. Here there's no suggestion of space, only flat, graphic surface. How did you decide on these backgrounds?

Sherman: It was fun making them, but it was also a lot of work. I fooled around with my computer and Photoshop when I first had a general idea for the background. That wound up being a challenge, because I didn't realize at first how much work that would entail. Later, I worked together with a technician on a much larger computer to make the transitions more fluent, so, for example, the hair looks more believable in front of the background.

Graw: And the colors you chose yourself, colors that by the way correspond to this season's (Summer 2004) "Day-Glo" fashion?

Sherman: Yes, I just experimented. I didn't think of fashion or a psychedelic aesthetic, however. I just explored what looked clown-like, what gives the impression of a funhouse. My method was just trying different things out.

Graw: Was this the first time that you experimented with digital image production?

Sherman: No, about two years ago I made similar, but much simpler backgrounds. For two pictures, one I call "Gardener-Girl" with a straw hat before an orange background, and she's wearing gardener's gloves. Another I call "Bimbo," she has long, blond curly hair and wears this really ugly blue disco dress and looks as if she's about to say, "Hi!" [Sherman says this with a high-pitched, flighty-sounding voice]. *The figures worked very well, but the original white backdrop looked boring and depressing. So I started experimenting on my laptop to find out what it would look like if the backgrounds were flooded in different colors.*

Graw: In your description of the characters you depict, it becomes clear how much you know about them, how precisely you study their habits. Do you seek out a certain type—like the "Gardener-Girl"—that you then, so to speak, fill? How is it that you decide not only to play a certain person, but also to slip into a character and to develop it in a certain way?

Sherman: Sometimes it develops linearly and organically. With "Gardener-Girl," for example, it started with a white farmer's shirt into which I'd sewn fake breasts: that had the advantage that I didn't have to affix any fake breasts onto my own body, I just had to slip into this blouse. At first she was a totally different type, had black hair and looked a bit like an Italian mama. After photographing this figure around five times, I slowly began adding things, like the straw hat. If something didn't work, I'd take another picture—like with jeans.

Graw: Did you have a certain image in your mind that you wanted to achieve, or was the process open ended?

Sherman: I never have anything in mind before I develop the film and look at the results. Then I think, for example, hmmm, what I originally wanted to do apparently didn't work. But here's something that interests me, maybe I should try going on in this direction. Then I break out in a new direction, experiment a bit and something else, unforeseen, excites my interest.

Graw: You begin with a certain experimental set-up and don't know what's going to come out in the end. Then you subject yourself to the process of editing: like a fashion editor who submits her own modeling performance to editing.

Sherman: Exactly.

Graw: What's your relationship to the facial expressions you make? I think that one can only convincingly present a facial expression when you mimetically absorb it, identify with it to a certain degree.

Sherman: Definitely. But I think that we all probably could identify with some aspects of them. But what I'm doing is superficial acting: I don't step into a figure and imagine how their life has been or where they live or what kind of family they have. I don't go that deep. For me, what I see in the mirror is much more decisive, and I attempt to change what I see in the mirror into something new and surprising for me.

Graw: You sit before the mirror and something unexpected comes to you from the mirror that you then have to do justice to. Could one then say that the audience is mainly yourself? Particularly in those clown works where you've assembled various figures, the clowns seem occupied with looking at themselves: even if they step out of the image, they're grinning at themselves. This reminds me of one of your earlier collages, *The Press Interviews the Director as the Actress Poses from the Murder Mystery Series* (1976), where you play the various actors of a fictive criminal case; you're both actress and director and seem to be looking at yourself in all these different roles. The beholder is banned, excluded from the event.

Sherman: The first thing I actually try to do is to entertain myself. When I work, it's supposed to be fun: not just during the work, but also afterward. I want to be the person who likes the results, and here I really don't care if the beholder likes it or not.

Graw: I'm also interested in the regressive vocabulary of your clown pictures that correspond, in my view, to the playful open character of your procedure. Here you're wearing a playsuit, there you're holding a teddy bear, or beating on a pot. This infantile repertoire can be read as an indication of a fundamentally regressive strain in your way of working.

Sherman: My decision for toys had more to do with the fact that clowns often entertain children. That's why there are strange things in the pictures, like the balloon animals. A child would point at it and say: look at this funny little thing. Many of the toys and props used by clowns are so silly and tiny.

Graw: The diptych that you showed in the gallery Metro Pictures (May 8–June 26, 2004) I liked because of the balloon dog being held by one of the figures and the balloon flowers affixed to the hat. I read the dog as a clear homage to Jeff Koons' balloon dog: it seems to represent a kind of low-tech version of it.

Sherman: Yes, the little dog is in fact supposed to be a reference to the Koons piece, which I rather like.

Graw: This object is held carefully by the clown figure as if it were a valuable, antique piece.

Sherman: Or as if the figure were proudly saying, "This is my little dog!"

Graw: In the catalog published by Thames & Hudson on your work, there are plans and sketches that show that you undertook certain guidelines and parameters, and proceeded systematically. At the same time, as we have seen, chance and unpredictability are productively mobilized. Can you describe this relationship between construction and coincidence more precisely?

Sherman: I try to let things go and I like it when things just happen coincidentally. That's why it's always easier for me to return to the use of my self. For when I work with dolls or mannequins, I must plan everything. Everything has to be ready for the moment when I take the picture; nothing can be left to chance. For one of those series, however, I did use the factor of chance by using different films. Either I took the shots using slide film and developed the negatives in different chemicals or I used print film that I then developed as a slide. The colors then changed completely depending on the film and the method of development. Those are the methods I used to force the element of chance onto this still life. By the way, one half of the diptych results from a coincidence. When I took the photo, I blinked. But the other versions with my eyes open didn't work for me.
But as important as it is to me that chance be given its place, I also think about the overall look of the series. As soon as I have photographed a few things, I begin analyzing them, making lists. If I have too many full-body shots, then I ask myself if I might need a few close-ups. I like it when things get mixed up, when everything differs. That's why I make these lists and plans.

Graw: You work also in series: and every series limits possibilities and is based on thematic premises. How do you come to these guidelines?

Sherman: In 2000 I shot the series that I called "Hollywood types." My idea for the characters was would-be or has-been actors (in reality secretaries, housewives, or gardeners) posing for headshots to get an acting job. These people are trying to sell themselves with all their might; they're just begging the viewer: don't you want to hire me? Two years after finishing this series I wanted to start working again. That was just after September 11. I photographed other types, still more women, but I had no idea of the direction that things were taking. It lacked structure. I gave up working and tortured myself for a while with the question of what to do.

Graw: And how did the clowns come up?

Sherman: When I'm trying to find inspiration, I usually clean up my studio and look through all the studio closets and drawers. I've collected so much stuff—props, costumes, and wigs. I dig about a bit and wait for something to inspire me. While doing that, I came upon some old pajamas that I had bought at a flea market. They were really old and falling apart, but someone had turned them into a clown's costume. I had never used them, but I thought that this might be a great thing to follow up on. Through research I realized that there are so many different clown looks that I could use just about anything, any old rags or combinations of clothing. There are clowns who just wear jeans and a garish T-shirt. Just because they wear a wig and white make-up, they're clowns. So I thought I'd found a very fertile subject.

Graw: When you stand before the mirror and experiment with various costumes, positions, and facial expressions, are you alone, or are assistants close by?

Sherman: I'm alone.

Graw: You alone in the studio—another modernist topos. Instead of corresponding to the image of the artist as an entrepreneur or a corporate director, your work points in a different direction. The image of the artist working alone in his or her studio is activated, the artist who acts processually, who allows him- or herself to make chance finds and knows how to use the relative autonomy of this site.

Sherman: Probably. I proceed like that because I work best that way. I've tried to work with other people—as an experiment—it never works. I'm not myself and tend to hold back. I don't drive other people the way I do myself. It seems to me I'm imposing on their time; even if I pay them, I want everything to work smoothly so that they can have fun, too.

Graw: Perhaps the situation is like when you're looking at yourself in the mirror and another person sees you doing it. That's always uncomfortable, as if you've gotten caught in an act of intimate self-reference. The facial expression that one makes before the mirror is not necessarily the one intended for the public, even if you're trying out a pose that you later show.

Sherman: It's just difficult for me to tell people what they have to do when I can't articulate it, because I have to see it first. I'm not necessarily a control freak, but I intuitively know what I want.

Graw: This knowledge can't be handed down or delegated, even though there are, of course, criteria for judging this; but they're difficult to communicate. Even Pollock couldn't delegate his dripping process.

Sherman: [laughing] *Yes, he couldn't explain to anyone else how to throw paint on the canvas.*

Graw: In comparison to your early film stills, the significance of situations has declined. In place of spatial situations or interiors, more abstract backgrounds have taken their place. I asked myself why you don't place the figures more in a setting. Could it be that situations and scenarios today are less interesting to you than psychic states?

Sherman: You mean, for example, [points at *Untitled Film Still* # 43, 1979]. *The background is not invented, she really sat there—in this tree. Even some of the interior shots are places where I myself lived. I just rearranged the furniture so that it looked like a stage set of an apartment. It's true, the setting is not so important to me anymore, at least not since the series from 2000 on. And in the case of the clowns, I wanted to give the impression of a background that could only be found in your head—or in their heads.*

Graw: At issue are representations of mental spaces?

Sherman: I guess so. While the Film Stills *were still narratively structured in the sense that there was a scenario, lately I'm just less interested in narrative. I've thought about incorporating it again, but it wouldn't look anything like the* Film Stills. *For the moment, I'm more interest in a headspace or entering psychic spaces, as if I were painting and simply inventing the spaces. Nothing has to make sense, you can just mix things up because they just look good together.*

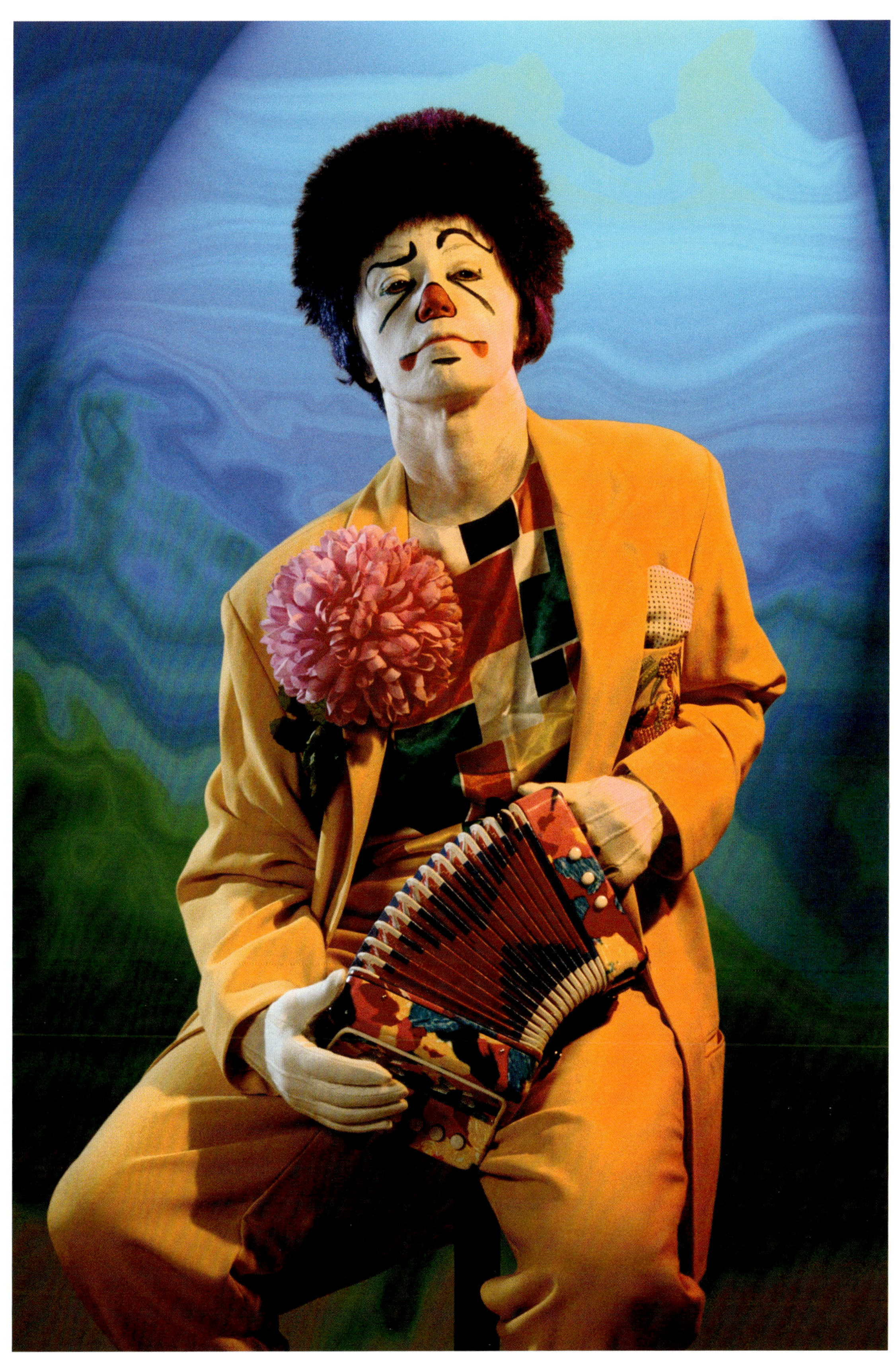

Untitled #423, 71¾ x 48½ in, 182.2 x 123.2 cm

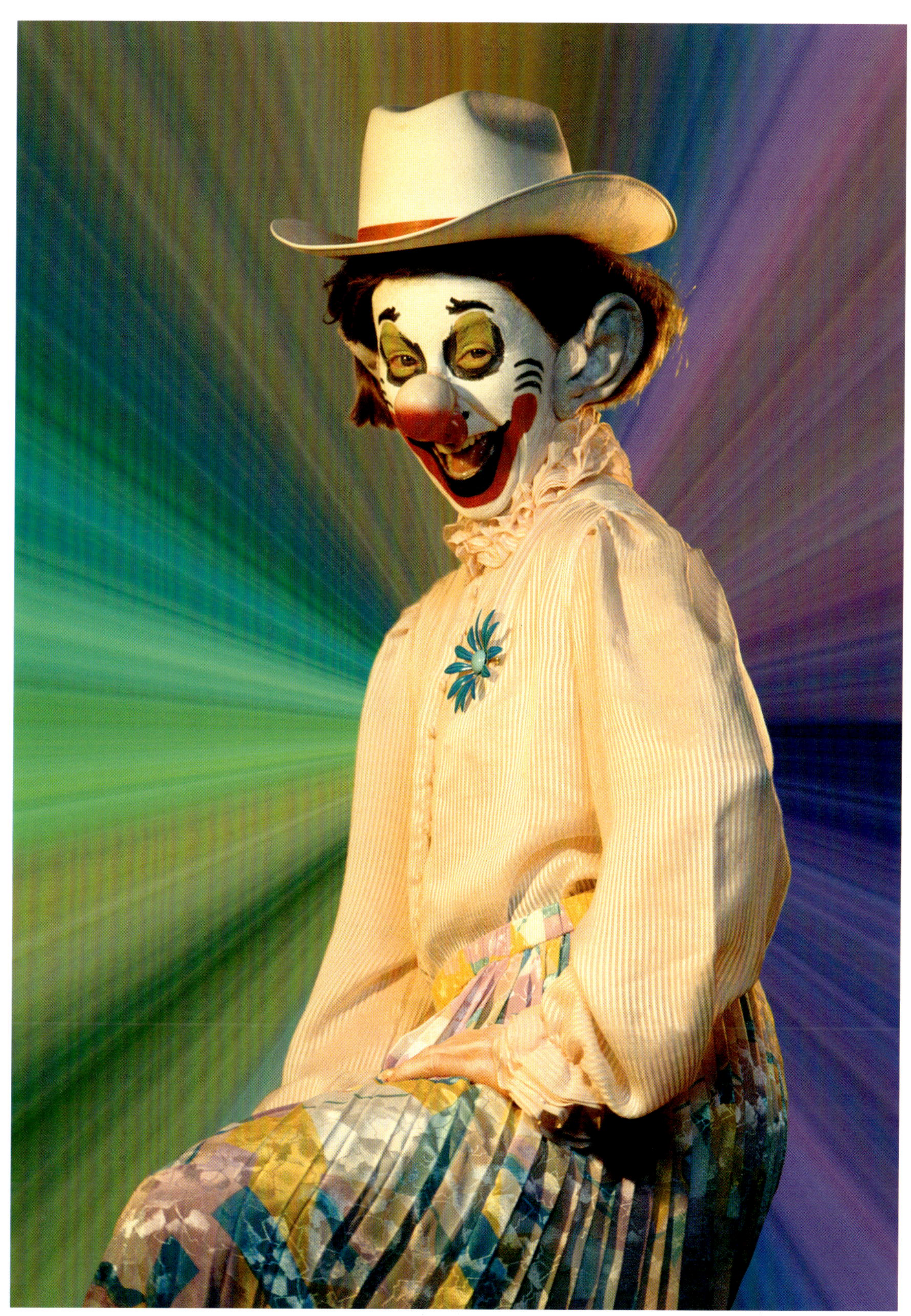

Untitled #410, 57 x 41¼ in, 144.8 x 104.8 cm

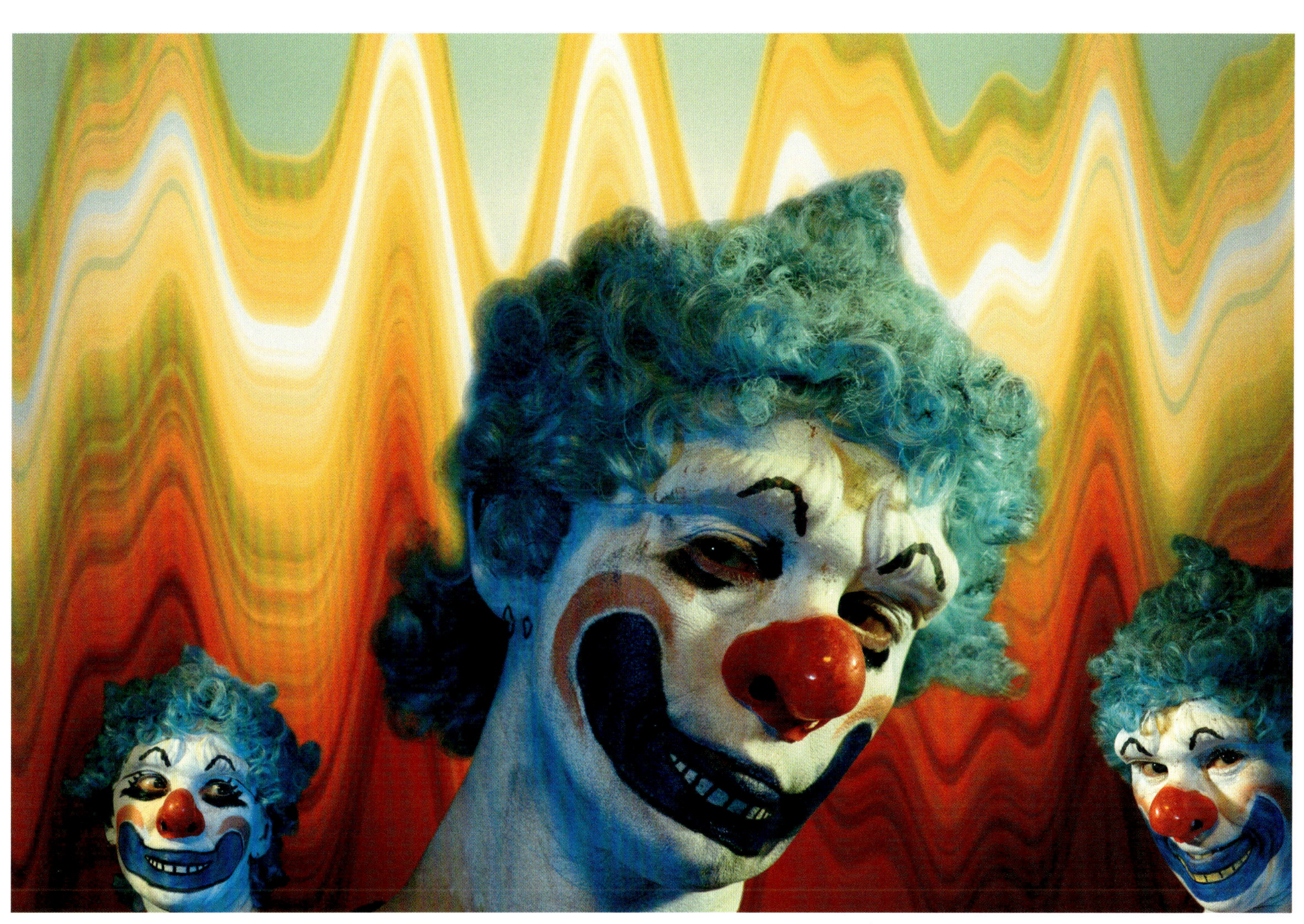

Untitled #417, 59¾ x 89½ in, 151.8 x 227.3 cm

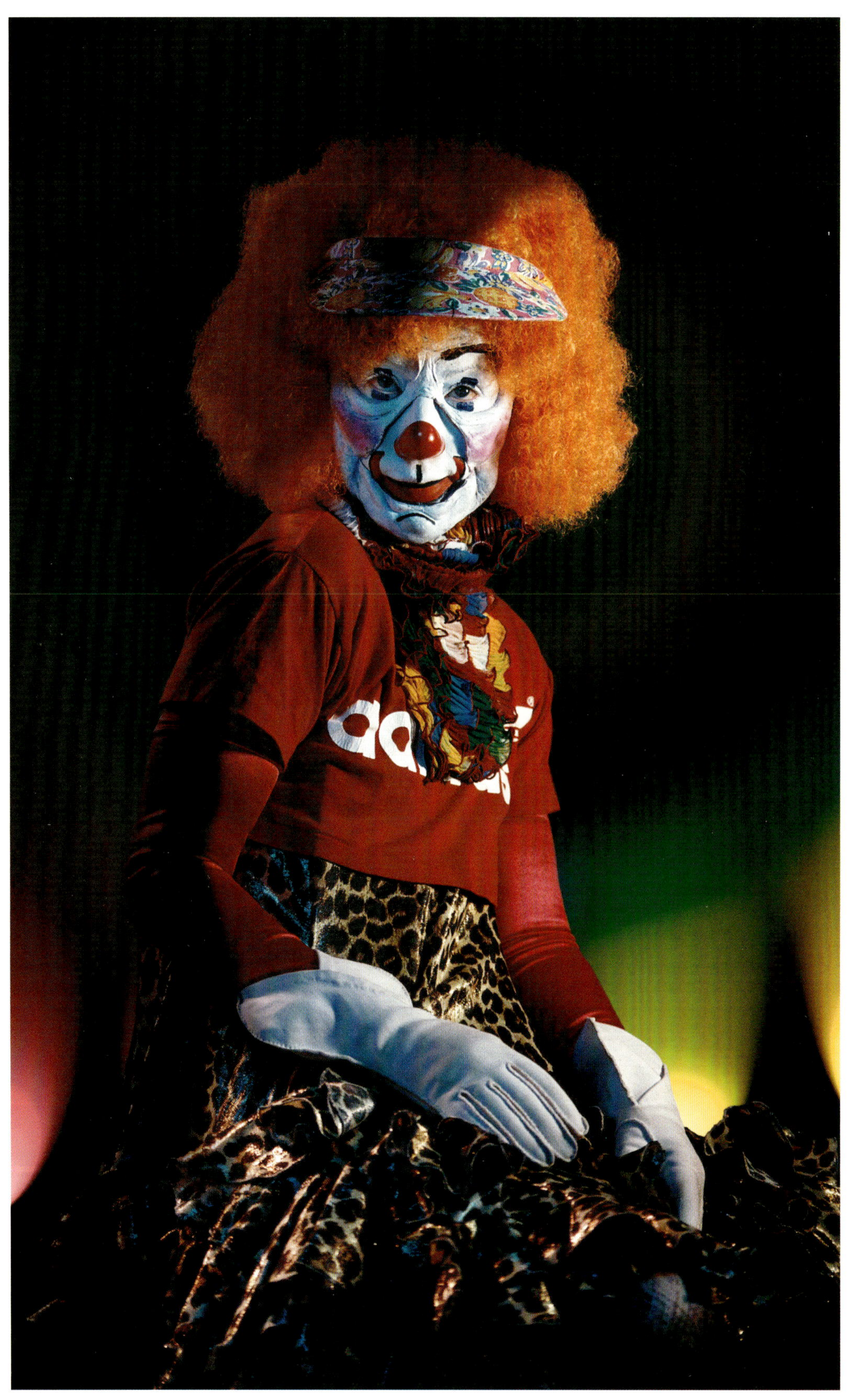

Untitled #418, 71¾ x 44¼ in, 182.2 x 112.4 x cm

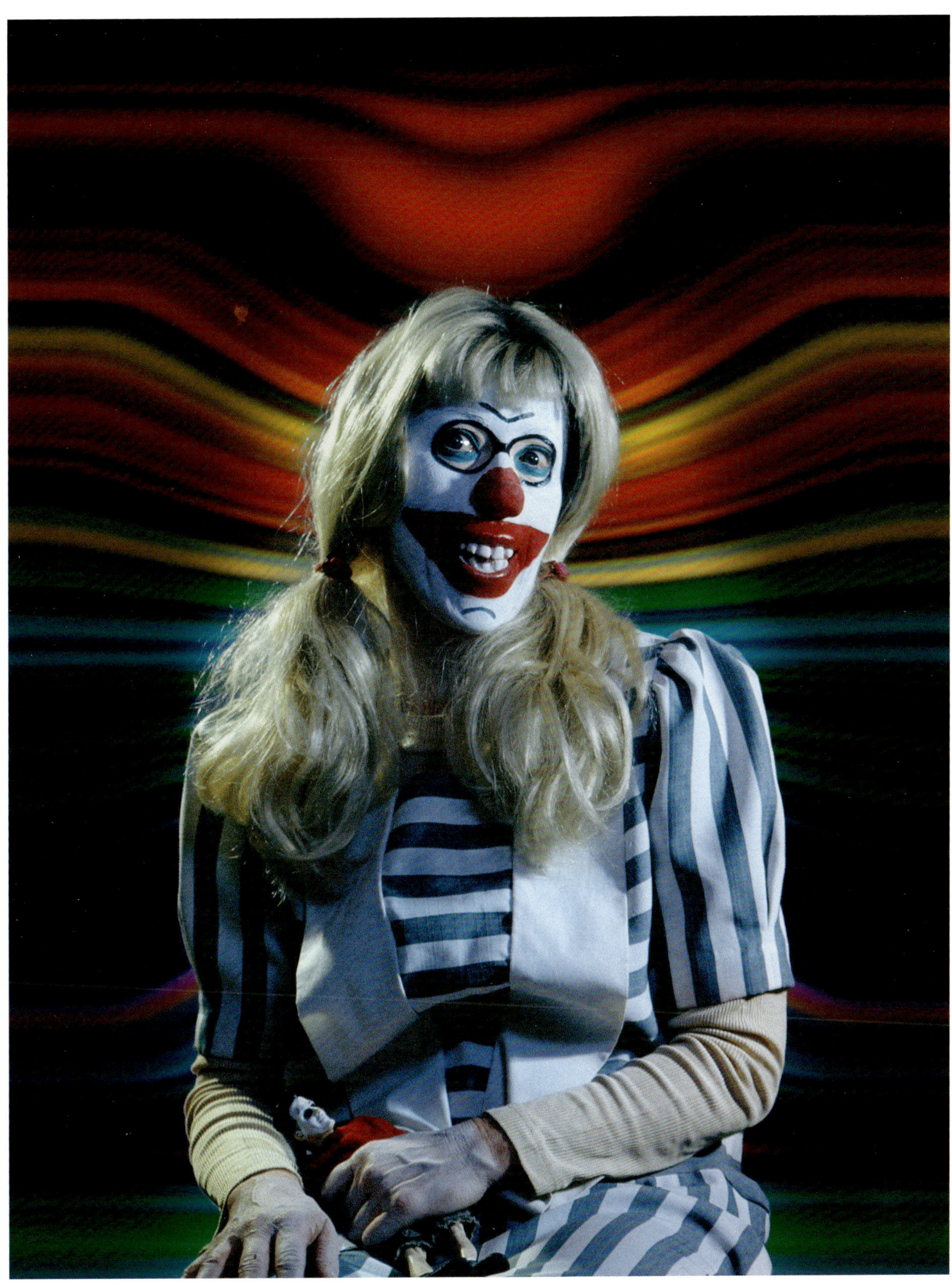

Untitled #412, 51¼ x 41¼ in, 130.2 x 104.8 cm

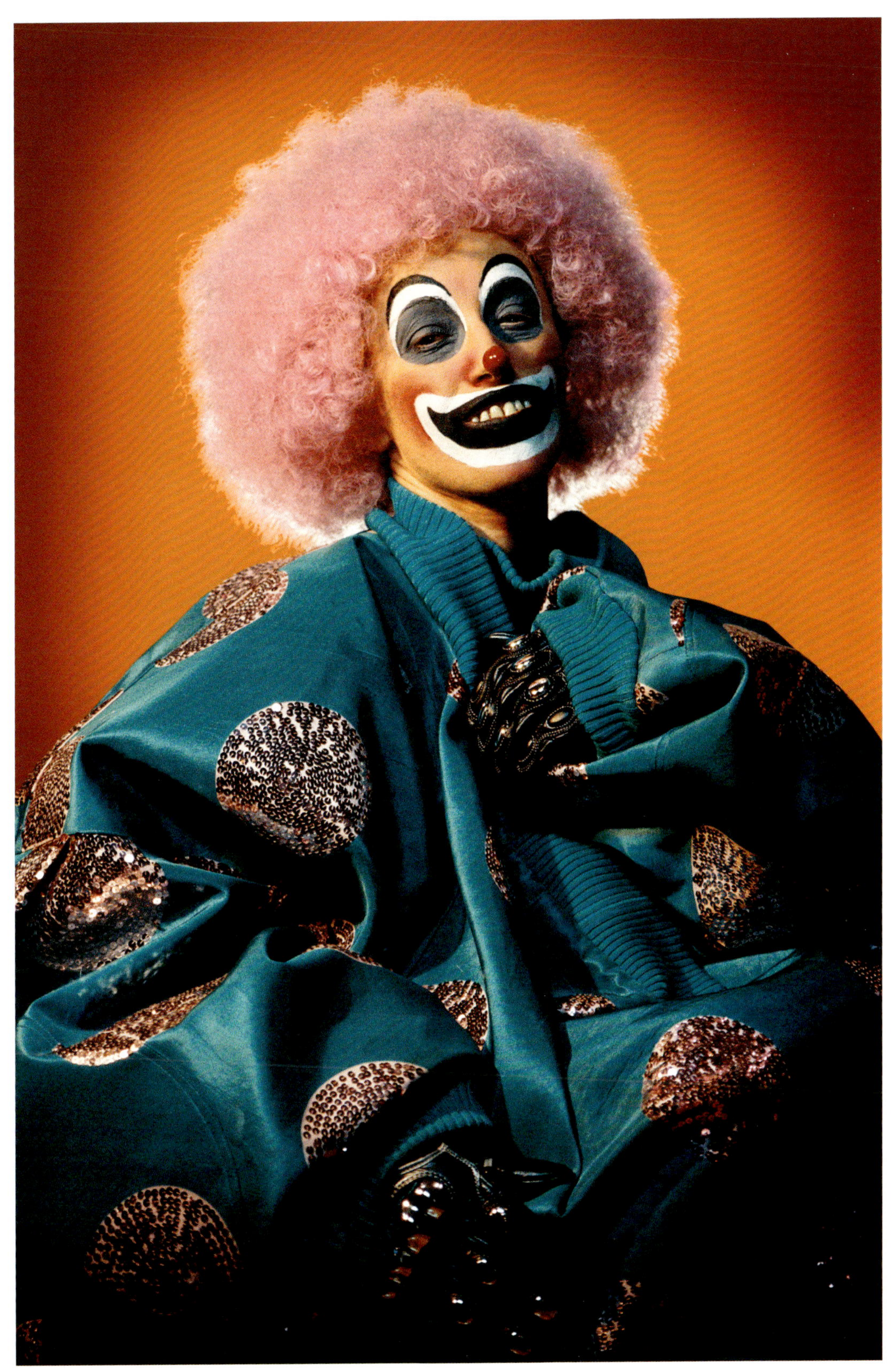

Untitled #414, 58 x 39¼ in, 147.3 x 99.7 cm

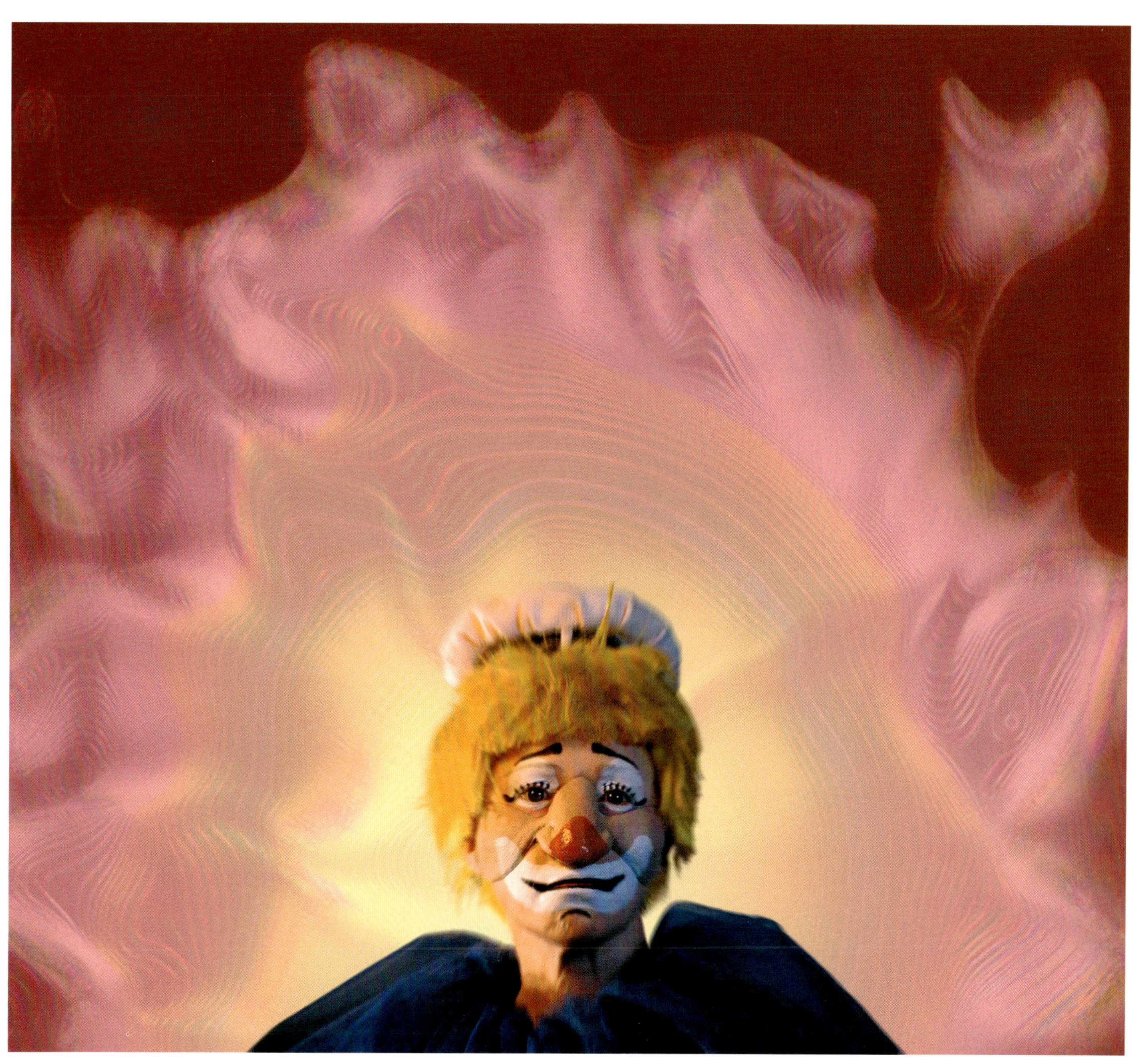

Untitled #422, 48½ x 54½ in, 123.2 x 138.4 cm

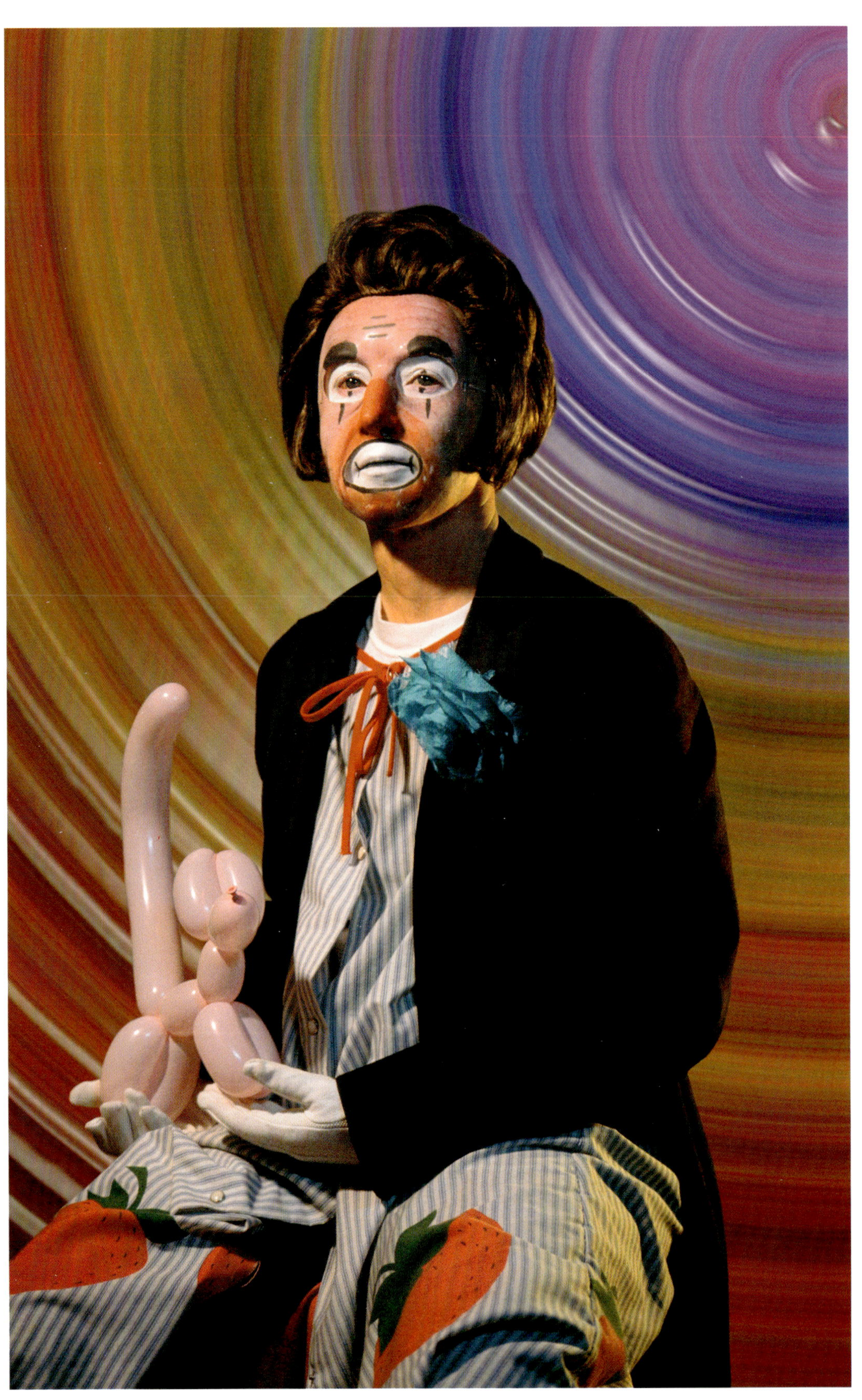

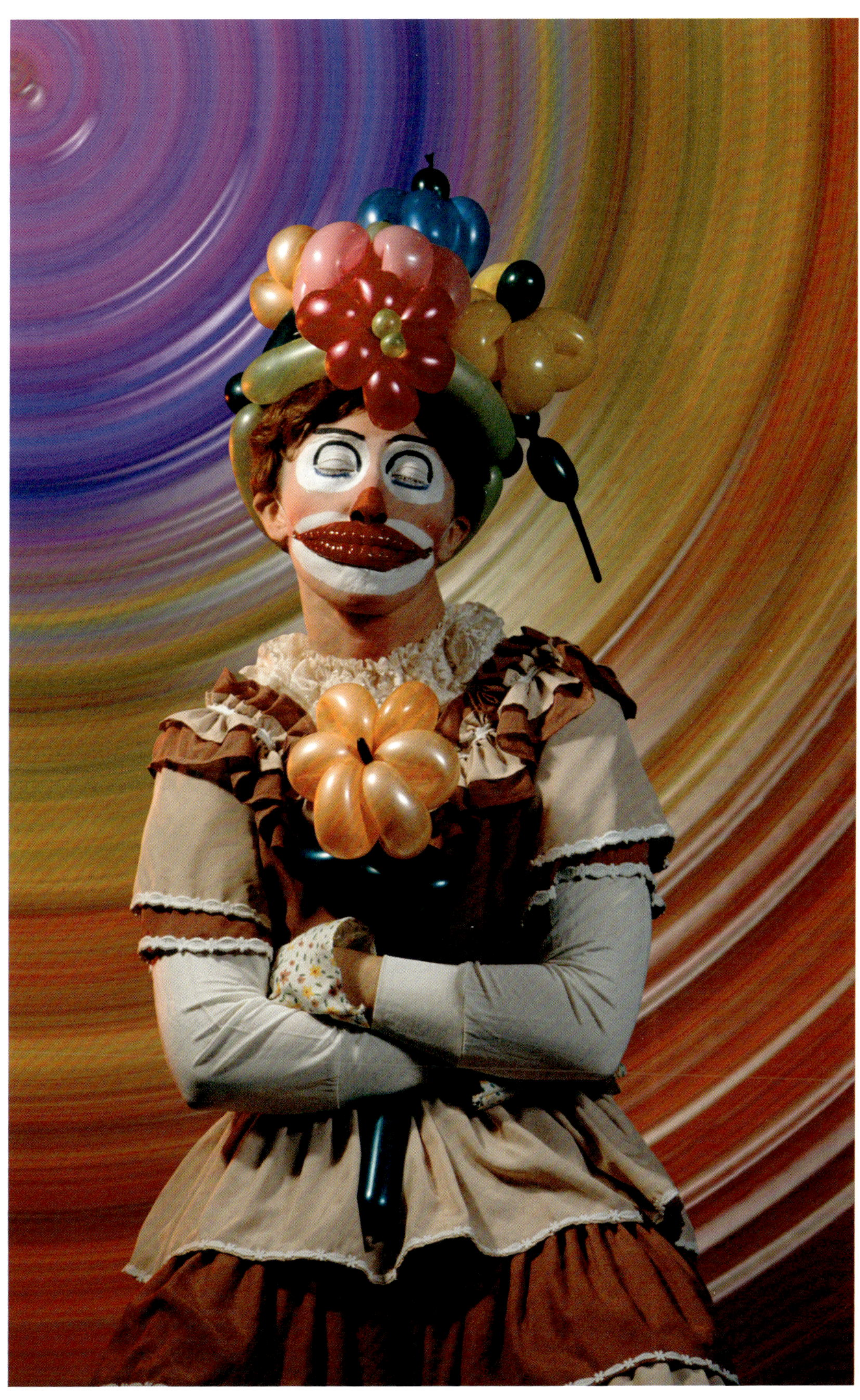

Untitled #420, each image 71¾ x 48½ in, 182.2 x 123.2 cm

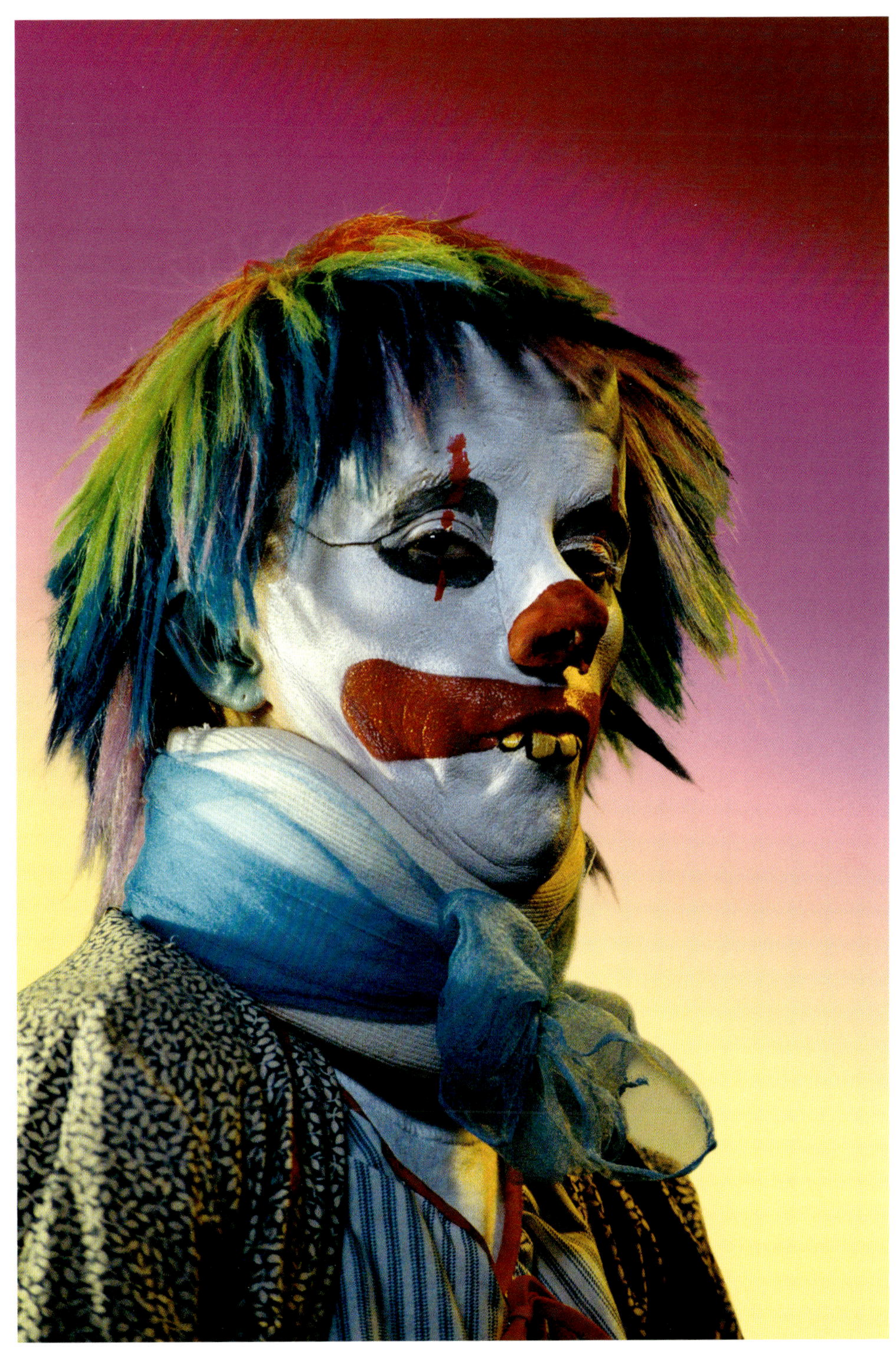

Untitled #411, 45¼ x 31⅛ in, 114.9 x 79.1 cm

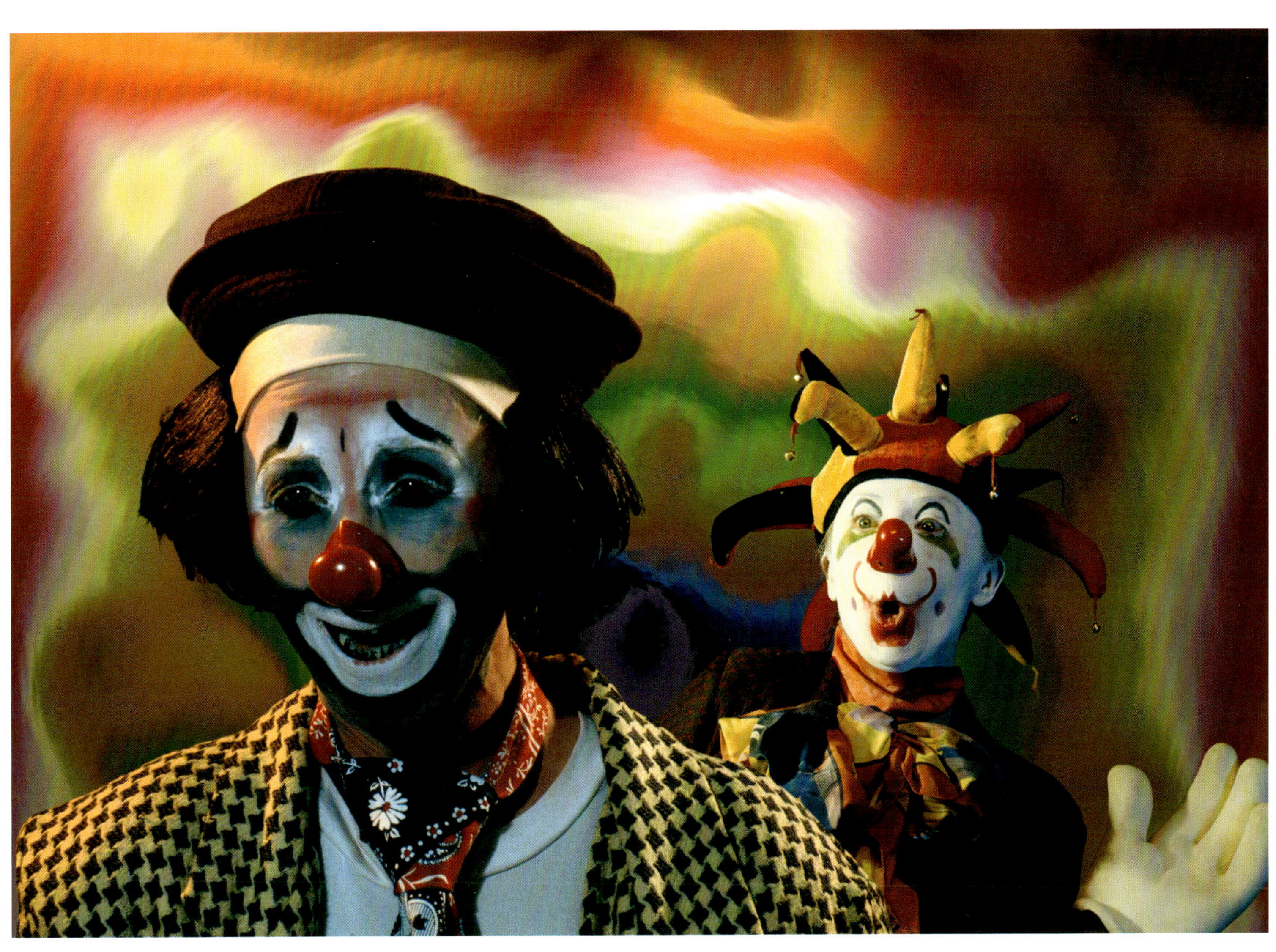

Untitled #421, 54¾ x 78¾ in, 139.1 x 200 cm

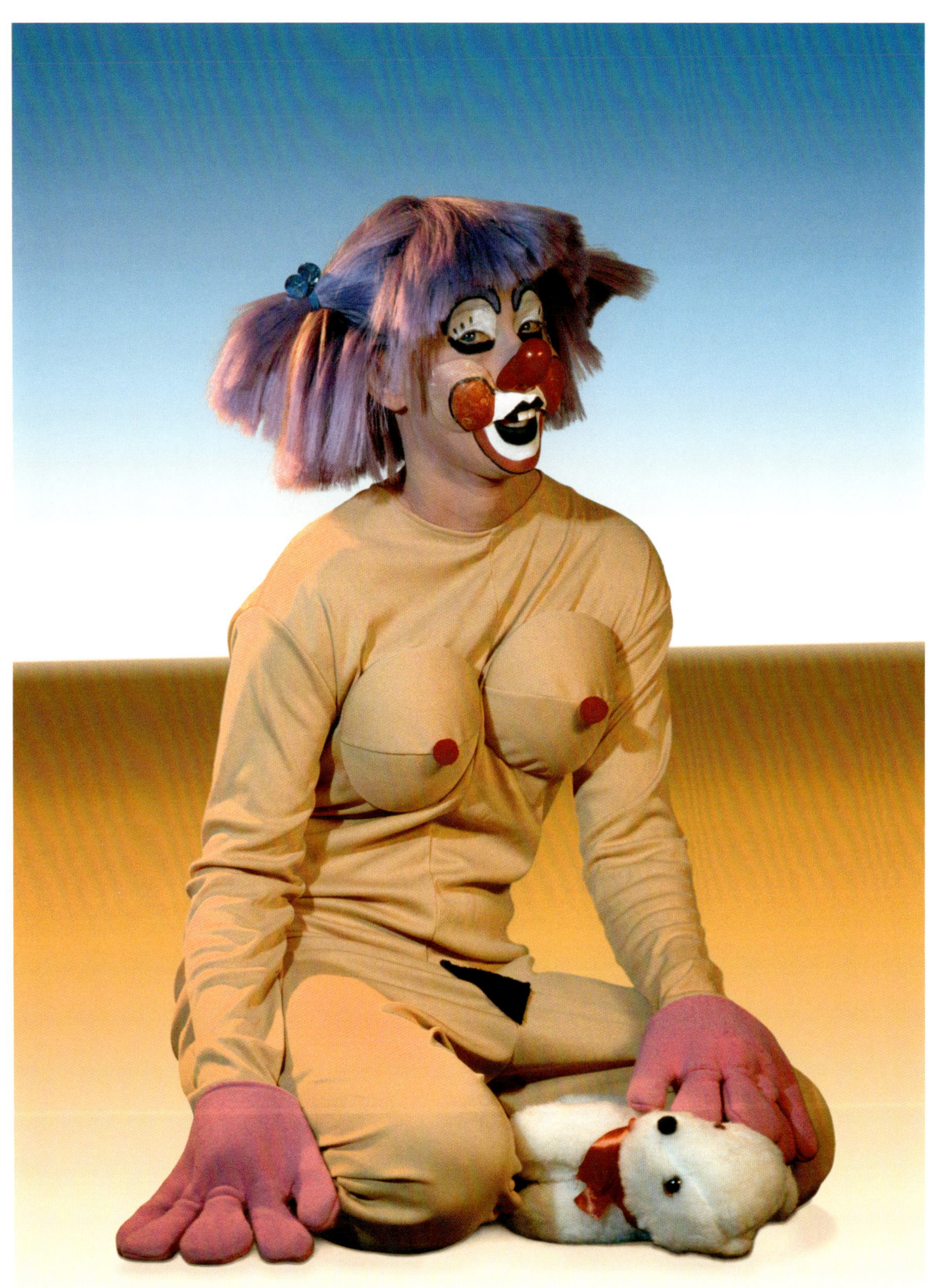

Untitled #419, 55½ x 48½ in, 141 x 123.2 cm

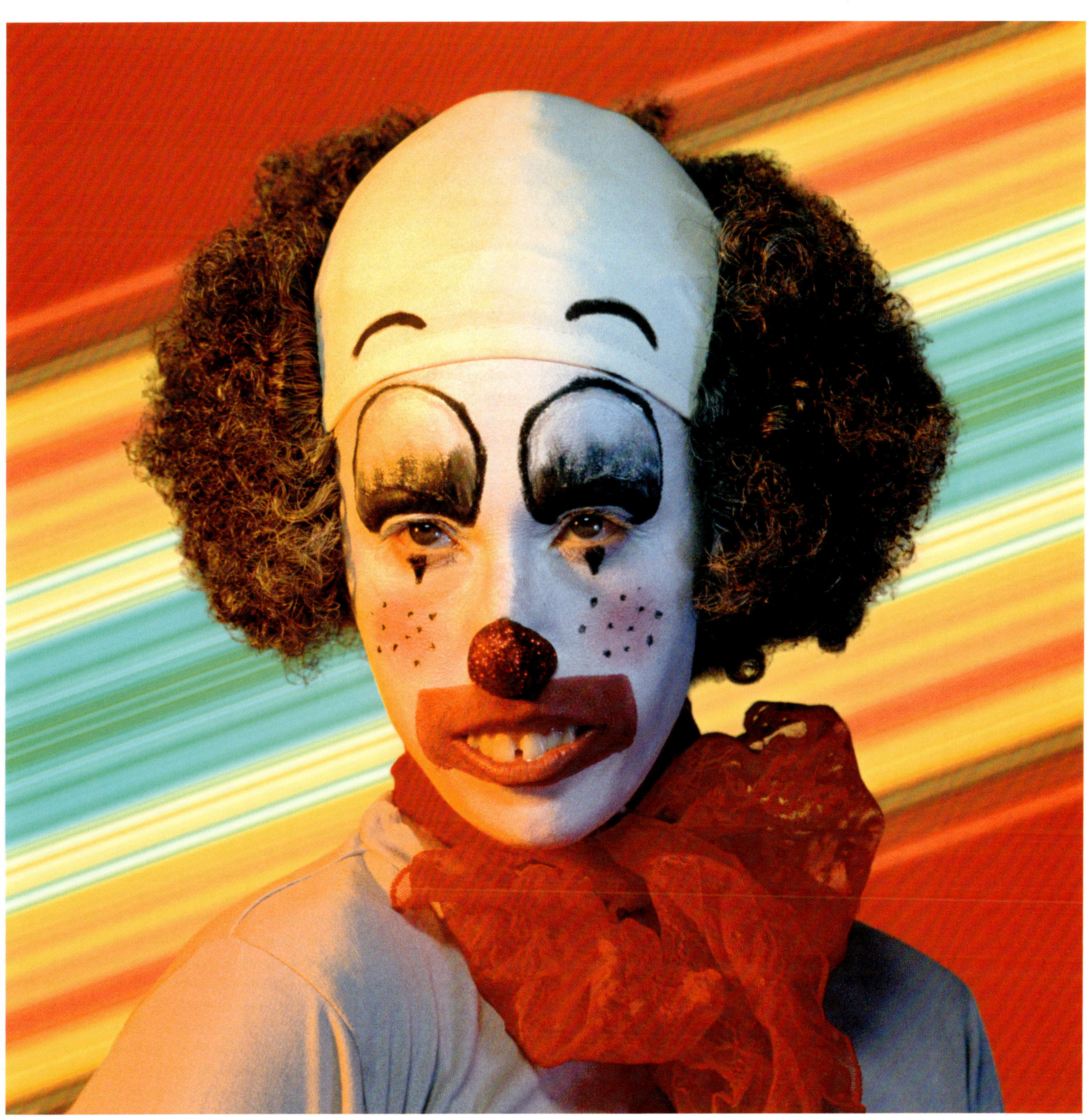

Untitled #424, 53¾ x 54¾ in, 136.5 x 139.1 cm

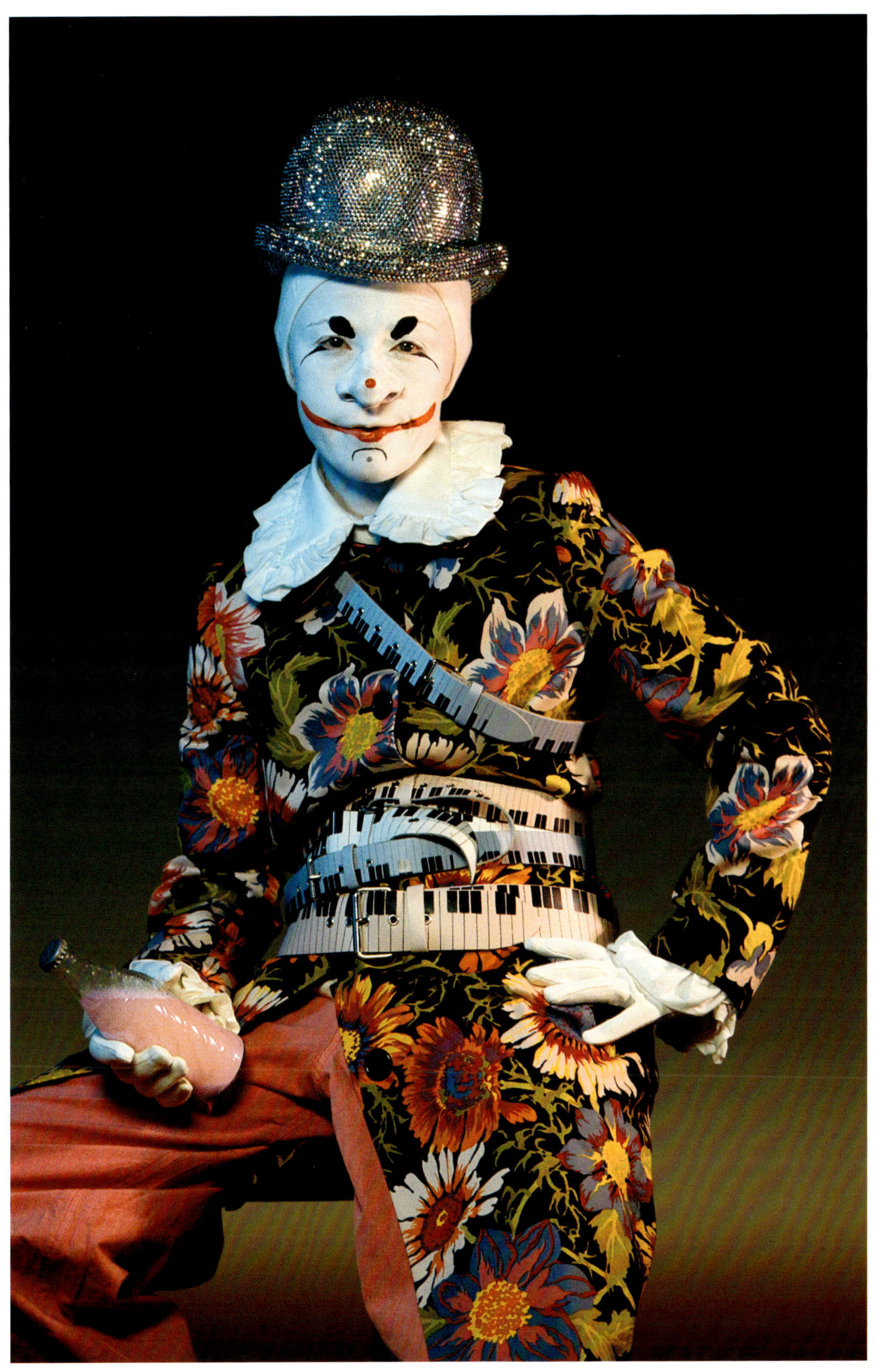

Untitled #415, 68 x 44½ in, 172.7 x 113 cm

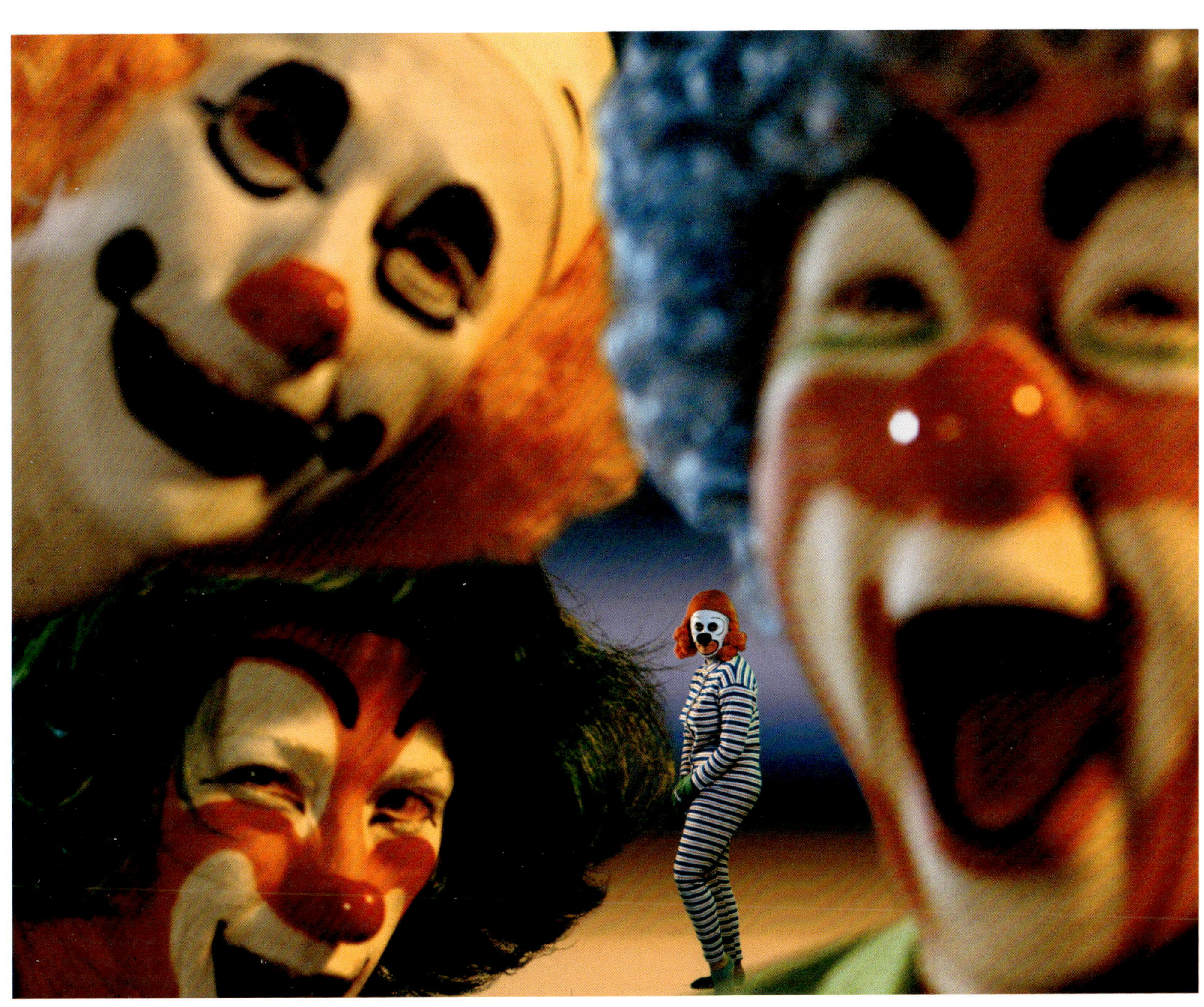

Untitled #425, 70¾ x 89¾ in, 179.7 x 228 cm

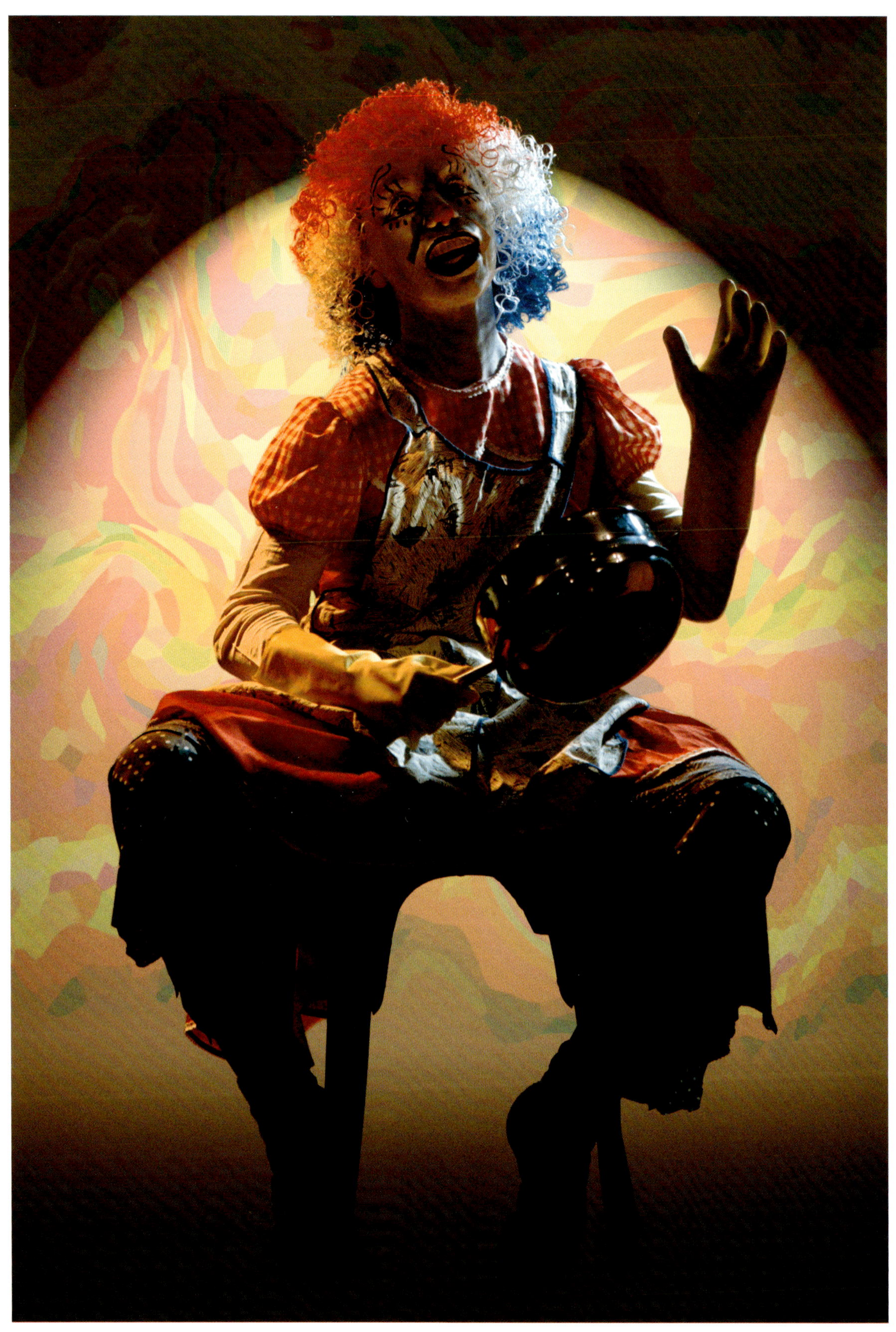

Untitled #426, 79½ x 55 in, 201.9 x 139.7 cm

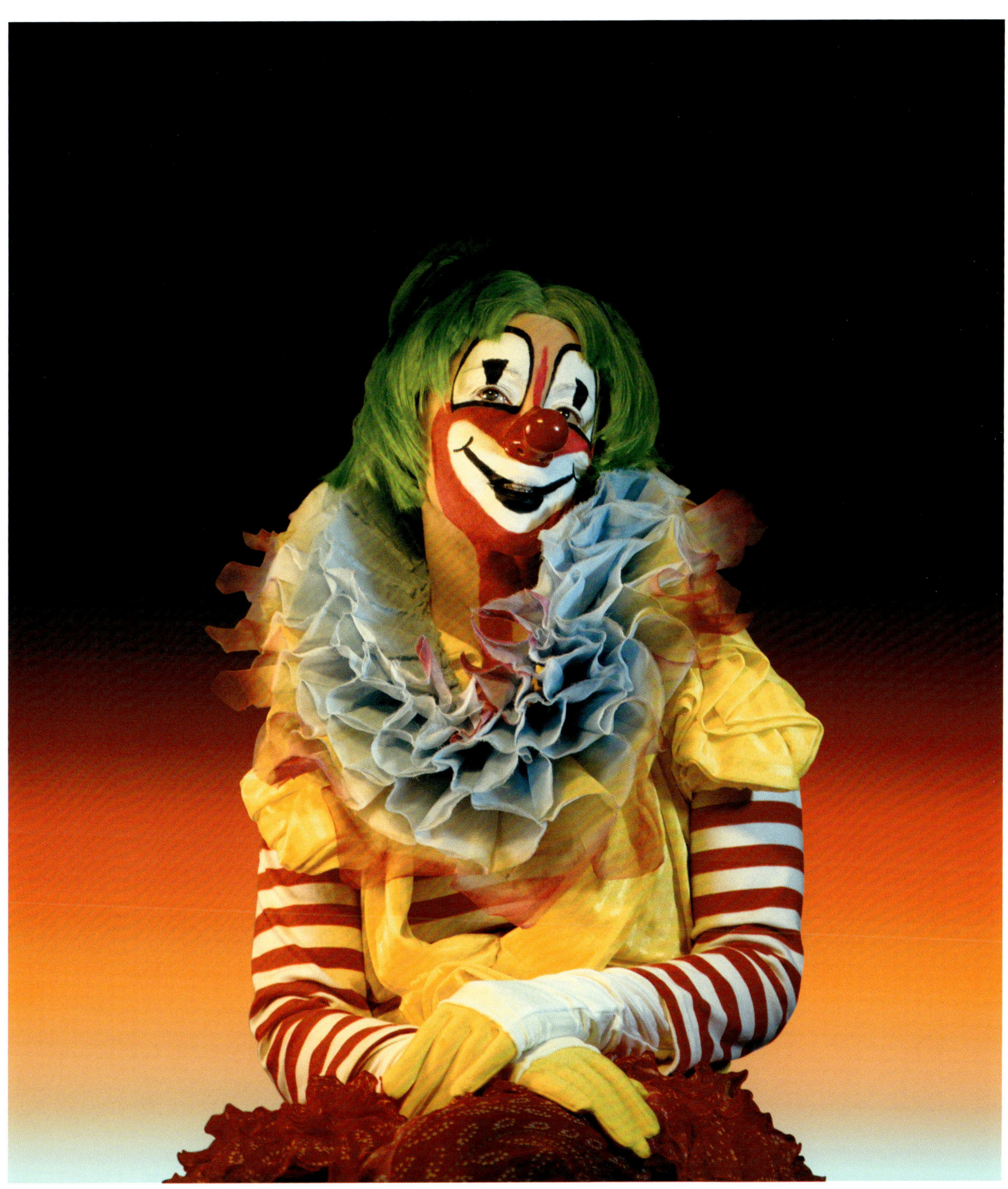

Untitled #416, 55¾ x 48 in, 141.6 x 123.2 cm

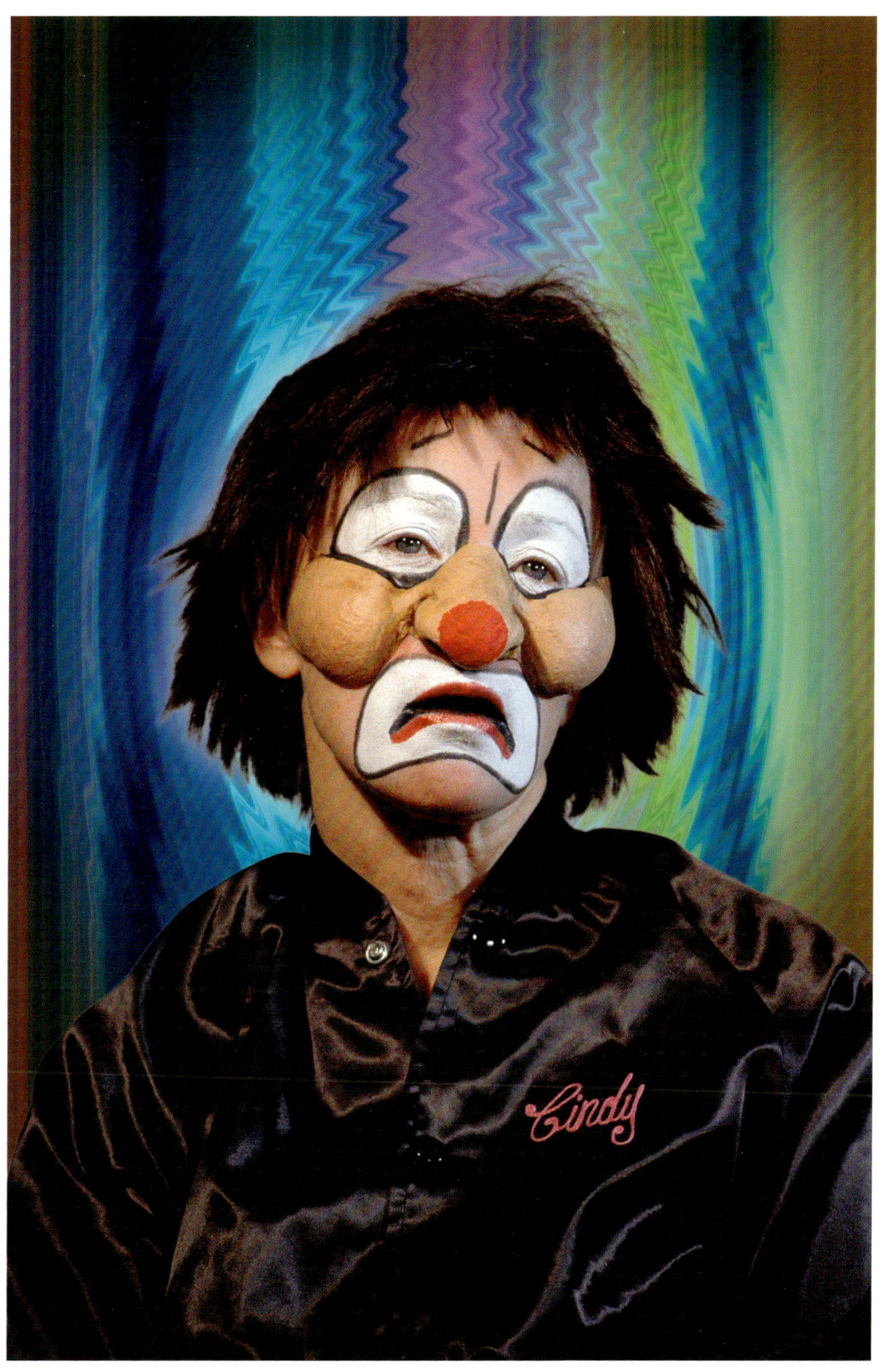

Untitled #413, 46 x 31⅛ in, 116.8 x 79.1 cm

VORWORT

Cindy Sherman gehört zweifellos zu den ganz großen und wichtigen Künstlerinnen unserer Zeit. Bereits seit ihrer frühen Arbeit, den *Untitled Film Stills* von 1977–80, hat sie sich mit Fragen der Identität und des Rollenwechsels beschäftigt. In ihren Serien war und ist Cindy Sherman immer beides: Künstlerin und Darstellerin. Auch in ihrer neuesten Serie, die in den letzen beiden Jahren entstanden ist, verbirgt sie sich selbst hinter der facettenreichen Maskerade des Clowns. Durch den Gebrauch digitaler Bildbearbeitungsprogramme ist es ihr möglich, sich selbst zu multiplizieren und als Personengruppe zu inszenieren. Gerade die kräftige Farbigkeit der ebenfalls digital erzeugten Hintergründe verdichtet die Intensität dieser grellen Travestie. Cindy Sherman gelingt es in ihrer Arbeit, immer neue, zeitgemäße Darstellungsformen zu finden und ihre Themen und Sujets kontinuierlich weiterzuentwickeln. Die hier publizierte Serie ist ein weiterer eindrucksvoller Beleg ihrer Kreativität als Künstlerin.

Wir sind sehr froh, die neuen Arbeiten von Cindy Sherman als erste Institution in Europa zeigen und mit einem monographischen Katalog begleiten zu können.

Mein größter Dank gilt daher Cindy Sherman für das Vertrauen und die Ehre, der kestnergesellschaft die Möglichkeit gegeben zu haben, die neue Werkreihe als Premiere zeigen zu können. Nicht unerheblichen Anteil daran hat Monika Sprüth, die als langjährige Galeristin der Künstlerin diese Ausstellung vermittelt und ermöglicht hat. Ihr und ihren Mitarbeitern gilt mein herzlicher Dank für die wie immer gute und professionelle Zusammenarbeit. Danken möchte ich auch Janelle Reiring und Helene Winer von Metro Pictures, der New Yorker Galerie der Künstlerin, für ihren Anteil am Gelingen dieser Ausstellung.

Den Katalog konnten wir glücklicherweise mit Lothar Schirmer machen, der ein ausgesprochener Kenner des Werks von Cindy Sherman ist und eine Reihe hervorragender Publikationen über ihre Arbeiten herausgegeben hat. Isabelle Graw möchte ich besonders dafür danken, daß sie bereit war, in New York ein Interview mit Cindy Sherman zu führen, das einen persönliche Einblick in die Arbeitsweise der Künstlerin wiedergibt. Schließlich danke ich Maik Schlüter, dem Kurator der Ausstellung für die sorgfältige Betreuung des Katalogs, seinen hervorragenden Text und die perfekte Inszenierung der Werke in unserem Haus.

Veit Görner, Direktor der kestnergesellschaft

SPASS, DER KEINER IST

Maik Schlüter

Der Clown wird als Statthalter einer ungetrübten Freude angesehen, ein aufgeschlossener Spaßmacher, der alle, insbesondere die Kinder, in seinen Bann zieht. Er ist der Trottel, der stellvertretend für das Publikum die Prügel bezieht und von einem Mißgeschick ins nächste stolpert. Immer unter den schadenfreudigen Blicken derer, die eigentlich selbst Opfer der Untiefen und Ungerechtigkeiten des Lebens sind. Clowns sind Projektionsflächen für den Spaß am Leid der anderen. Dieses Leid wird mal als melancholische Geste, als hintergründige Ironie oder als platter Slapstick inszeniert. Das Spektrum seiner Aktivitäten reicht von der Darstellung des ernsten und traurigen Verlierers über den stillen und wundersamen Zauberer bis hin zum lauten Anarchisten, der alle Regeln auf den Kopf stellt. Alle diese Charaktere haben etwas Widersprüchliches, stimulieren sie doch einerseits die positiven Seiten der Gefühlswelt, verleiten zum Lachen und zum Staunen, und verweisen andererseits auf die Grenzen und Repressionen der Normalität und weiter auf die Unvollständigkeit und Unwägbarkeit der Welt. Im Spaß wird immer auch die Tragik des Lebens umkreist. Dem Clown haftet zudem etwas Undurchdringliches an, trägt er doch eine massive und obszöne Fratze zur Schau und stilisiert jede seiner Handlungen. Man weiß nie genau, in welche unterirdische Falle er tappen und wer das nächste Opfer seiner Scherze werden wird. Gerade der Widerspruch zwischen der fröhlichen Grimasse und der Durchtriebenheit und Unberechenbarkeit seiner Handlungen macht den Reiz dieser schillernden Figur aus. Letztlich verbirgt sich hinter der farbenfrohen Maske der Tod, der unvorhergesehen und brutal, unabänderlich und konsequent die Welt und die Menschen regiert. Die Wahrheit ist doppelbödig: In der Kraft des Lachens liegt die Überwindung der Angst und des Verlustes, gleichzeitig manifestiert sich darin der hilflose Versuch, dem Unabänderlichen etwas entgegenzusetzen. Aber auch in einem kleineren Maßstab klärt der Clown auf und zeigt dem Publikum, ähnlich wie der Hofnarr dem König, die abgeschwächte Version seiner Unzulänglichkeiten und Fehler. Aber wie der Herrscher erträgt auch der Rest der Gesellschaft sich selbst nur im Zerrspiegel clownesker Unterhaltung. Es geht um Kanalisierung, nicht um Veränderung, nicht die aufklärende Erkenntnis über den Status quo steht im Mittelpunkt, sondern lediglich seine Aufweichung und Abschwächung. Das Ziel ist, die Bedingungen und inneren Konstellationen erträglicher zu machen.

In Cindy Shermans neuer Arbeit von 2003/2004 erscheint der Clown als grelles Abziehbild einer aufgesetzten und falschen Fröhlichkeit. Jedes Lächeln, jede theatralische Geste ist entweder durchsetzt von abgründiger Bösartigkeit, von hilfloser Einsamkeit, debiler Einfalt oder vordergründiger Sexualisierung. Sherman folgt innerhalb dieser neuen Arbeit ihren bereits in anderen Werken ausformulierten Interessen: gesellschaftliche Rollenzuschreibungen, unterdrückte Lüste, Ängste und Gewalttätigkeiten aufzuzeigen und immer wieder die Frage zu thematisieren, wie die Bilder dieser gesellschaftlichen Tatsachen aussehen. Sherman zeigt nicht den traurigen Pierrot. Sie zeigt nicht den Skeptiker oder Melancholiker, dem alles Scheitern in der Welt bewußt ist und der trotzdem oder gerade deswegen versucht, sein Publikum zu unterhalten, und der dann seine Tränen verbirgt. Wir sehen vielmehr die überzogene und kommerzielle Version des Clowns.

Ein schreiendes und aggressives Make-up verwandelt ihn in eine exzentrische Ausgeburt permanenter und vor allem penetranter Fröhlichkeit. Ein Marktschreier, Ronald McDonald eben, der die Kinder bezirzt und die Eltern erpreßt: „Wollt ihr wirklich wegen ein paar Dollar mehr, die unser Fastfood und Billigspielzeug kostet, eure Kinder von dieser Geburtstagsparty wegziehen? Ganz bestimmt nicht, oder?“

Aber Clowns können mehr, sie sind nicht nur Multiplikatoren und Aufreißer der Werbung, sie sind auch fester Bestandteil der Zirkuskultur. Wir wissen allerdings, wie wenig das romantische Bild vom herumfahrenden Artisten zutrifft. Statt freier Liebe und poetischer Inspiration gilt es, harte Arbeit, wenig Geld und Ansehen auszuhalten. Im Falle des Clowns bedeutet dies, professionell lustig zu sein, spontan und doch kontrolliert das zu zeigen, was die Leute sehen wollen: sich selbst und doch jemand anderen. Aber das Spiel mit dem Stellvertreter ist gefährlich, ist es doch durchsetzt von einer grundsätzlichen Unehrlichkeit. Nicht der ganze Mensch wird gezeigt, sondern lediglich sein lächerliches und abgeflachtes Abziehbild. Abgrund und Größe bleiben verborgen, entschärft ist die Tragweite und Tragik menschlichen Handelns. Für den Clown und sein Repertoire bedeutet dies, daß die Gummikeule eigentlich ein Fallbeil oder Maschinengewehr, der weggezogene Stuhl und das lustige Ärgern die Entsprechung der Folter ist und jedes am-Boden-Liegen einem sexuellen Übergriff, einem Akt der Gewalt nahekommt. Freilich ist seine oberflächliche Zärtlichkeit auch ein Ausdruck möglicher Sympathie und Liebe. Aber davon sprechen die Clowns der Cindy Sherman nicht. Böse und verzerrt sind die Masken, und Sherman zeigt uns Clowns, die geil und sadistisch, gemein und unergründlich, brutal und verlogen sind. Sie

zeigt eine Welt, die voller Tücken und Widersprüche ist, und produziert ein Lachen, das im Halse steckenbleibt. Bilder, deren Wirkung nicht ausbleibt und die zeigen, wie albern und einfältig der Wunsch nach „clownesker" Unterhaltung ist. Der Widerspruch, der sich im traurigen Pierrot zeigt, tritt bei Sherman härter zutage und wird auf die Spitze getrieben.
Shermans Clowns lassen sich auch im Zusammenhang mit anderen zeitgenössischen Arbeiten lesen, wie z.B. *Clown Torture* (1987) von Bruce Nauman, der in einer beklemmenden Installation die immer gleichen, entleerten und hilflosen Gesten und Worte der grellen Spaßmacher zeigt und offen läßt, wer von wem gefoltert wird; Paul McCarthys *Painter* (1995), der den Maler als begriffslose Witzfigur präsentiert, die rein zufällig zu einem respektablen und kreativen Ergebnis kommt und obendrein vom Publikum kaum ernst genommen wird; Jonathan Borofskys *The Dancing Clown at 2,845,325* (1982/83), eine unheimliche und monströse Hybride aus Ballerina und Clown, die anmutig und tragisch, traurig und lächerlich zugleich erscheint; oder Ugo Rondinones zusammengesackte und fette Clowns (*If There Were Anywhere But Desert: Tuesday*, 2002), die erschöpft am Boden sitzen oder liegen – traurige Varietékünstler, die ausgelaugt sind vom ständigen Spagat zwischen guter Laune und innerem Abgrund, zwischen Geifer und Applaus.
Alle diese Arbeiten zeigen nicht den Clown als Künstler, sondern den Künstler als Clown, verweigern aber eine positive Identifikation im Sinne des sensiblen Außenseiters oder närrischen Aufklärers. Bei McCarthy drückt der Maler aus einer übergroßen Tube mit der Aufschrift „SHIT" die Farbe auf die Palette und beginnt anschließend, in seinem merkwürdig isoliert wirkenden Studio die Leinwand vollzuschmieren. Das ist hohe Kunstpraxis und ihre Rezeption: Fiktive Fähigkeiten und Werte werden kreiert, die Kunst ist nicht mehr als ein Ergebnis von Spekulationen und der Künstler oder die Künstlerin ein willfähriger Idiot, der in der Analphase seiner Persönlichkeitsentwicklung steckengeblieben ist. Wenn die Show und vor allem die Stereotypen vom verantwortungslosen und unreflektierten Künstler stimmen, läßt sich alles verkaufen und das Publikum hat die Kunst dort, wo es sie haben will: am Rande der Gesellschaft, als anarchische und allenfalls dekorative Unterhaltung. Ähnliches können wir bei Nauman, Borofsky, Rondione oder Sherman sehen. Die Figur des Künstlers oder der Künstlerin ist nie ganz ernst zu nehmen, sie hat eine definierte und begrenzte Rolle zu spielen, als tragikomischer Held, der sich mit Merkwürdigkeiten und spleenigen Ideen beschäftigt und dessen Ergebnisse deshalb nicht nachvollziehbar sind, weil die Kunst von vornherein nicht als zentrale Größe des gesellschaftlichen Lebens gedacht

wird, sondern immer nur als Ausdruck von unterhaltsamem, kontemplativem oder irrationalem Luxus, der allenfalls mit abgründigen und verdrängten Gefühlen einhergeht. Und da treffen sich die Erwartungen, die an den Clown und den Künstler/die Künstlerin gleichermaßen herangetragen werden: ein Stellvertreter für das unausgelebte Gefühlsleben des Publikums sein zu müssen. Eine Figur, deren Aussagen und Handlungen immer unter der Firnisschicht der künstlerischen Verklärung wahrgenommen werden und die damit weit genug vom eigenen Leben entfernt sind, um als tatsächliche Kritik gelesen zu werden.

Cindy Sherman widerspricht an dieser Stelle und gibt dem Zuschauer, was er verdient: sich selbst als Idioten und bösartigen Conférencier sehen zu müssen, der nicht darauf hoffen kann, daß die Kunst ihn beruhigt oder ablenkt. Es ist das Spiel mit der Maskerade, das Sherman dafür wählt. Und warum dieses Spiel nicht ganz direkt als Metapher des sozialen Lebens lesen, als Strategie der Verunsicherung, als freundlich-falsches Bild, das über die niedrigen Intentionen im gesellschaftlichen Miteinander hinwegtäuschen will? Oder weniger allgemein, als sexualisierte und gewalttätige Maske, die für den Moment der sogenannten Perversion die Identität verschleiert oder ersetzt und dem oder der TrägerIn erlaubt, im Namen eines anderen zu ficken, zu schlagen, zu quälen oder subtilere Formen der Beherrschung und der Unterdrückung zu finden. Die Maske als Ausdruck der täglich gelebten, schizoiden Doppelbödigkeiten und Widersprüche. Der Clown wird so zum Sinnbild der Entfremdung. Cindy Sherman benutzt das mimische Repertoire an Abgründigem und steigert einmal mehr die Angst/Lust-Phantasien des Publikums. Auch wenn die Show weitergeht, am Ende gilt: Gelacht wird darüber, daß es nichts zu lachen gibt.

OHNE MAKE-UP

Ein Interview mit Cindy Sherman von Isabelle Graw

Graw: Ich wollte Dir vorschlagen, daß wir über Dein künstlerisches Verfahren sprechen, wobei ich nicht Deinem authentischen Verfahren auf der Spur bin, sondern dem Verfahren, das in Deiner Arbeit *suggeriert* wird. Es kommt mir so vor, als würde für jede Serie eine Versuchsanordnung mit bestimmten Parametern aufgestellt. In diese Festlegung spielen dann aber auch Zufall und Willkür hinein. Mich interessiert, inwieweit Du diese Kontingenzen aufsuchst und provozierst. Nehmen wir Deine frühe Arbeit *Bus riders* (1976/2000) mit ihrer gleichbleibenden Versuchanordnung: ein Stuhl, ein sichtbares Kabel, eine bestimmte räumliche Situation. Das, was in ihr geschieht, hat jedoch eine gewisse Eigendynamik – verschiedene Typen werden durchgespielt. Du hast sie auf Dich genommen, gestaltest sie, überläßt Dich ihnen aber auch.

Sherman: Wenn Du „überlassen“ sagst, meinst Du damit eine Form der Selbstaufgabe?

Graw: Ja – Selbstaufgabe als künstlerische Methode. Das ist ja im Grunde genommen ein altes modernistisches Thema. Nur gingen modernistische Kritiker wie Clement Greenberg davon aus, daß z.B. das Material gewisse Vorgaben mache, denen der Künstler Folge zu leisten habe, so als wären diese Vorgaben gegeben. Ich würde es weniger normativ und als produktionsästhetische Notwendigkeit formulieren und sagen, daß sich Künstler in der Regel bestimmten Vorgaben überlassen, für die sie sich allerdings entschieden haben. Der „Clown“-Topos Deiner neuen Arbeiten ist ja zum Beispiel kunsthistorisch überdeterminiert. Ich muß gestehen, daß ich normalerweise heftige Aversionen gegen Clowns und gegen alles, was sie konnotieren, hege – die Maske oder das Klischee vom „traurigen Clown.“

Sherman: Das geht, glaube ich, allen Leuten so, speziell in diesem Land [USA].

Graw: Wieso?

Sherman: Ein Clown, der in Paris an einer berühmten Clownschule studiert hat, sagte mir, daß diese Abneigung gerade in Amerika besonders ausgeprägt sei und zwar wegen der vielen Clowns, die hier in Werbung, Kindersendungen und ähnlichem benutzt werden und immer schrecklicher und beängstigender geworden sind. Man sieht Clowns hier nicht als eine Kunstform an, was in Europa anders ist.

Graw: Von Picasso-Bildern bis hin zu Fellini-Filmen: Der Clown eignet sich als künstlerische Projektionsfläche. Als ich mir Deine Clown-Bilder angesehen habe, fragte ich mich jedoch, ob ich es tatsächlich mit Clowns zu tun habe. Gibt es Clowns, die sich auf derart grotesk-monströse Weise Zähne auf den Mund malen? Mir kam es so vor, als hättest Du die Vorgabe „Clowns" nur benutzt, um deren Konventionen zu sprengen und viel weiter zu gehen.

Sherman: Ja – ich wollte nicht einfach nur traditionelle Portraits von Clowns machen. Mir ging es darum, die Sache weiterzutreiben. Aber es gibt tatsächlich Clowns, die aufgemalte Zähne haben... Ich habe mich an Darstellungen von Clowns orientiert, die ich in Büchern oder im Internet gefunden habe. Die größte Herausforderung bestand für mich darin, eine Persönlichkeit unter dem Make-up des Clowns hervortreten zu lassen – eine Persönlichkeit, die nichts mit meiner eigenen zu tun haben würde. Mir war es wichtig, daß jede dieser Persönlichkeiten anders aussehen würde – ich wollte sozusagen etwas hinter dem Make-up finden, etwas Fremdes, das hindurchscheint.

Graw: Das Format „Clowns" erlaubte es Dir auch, keinen Zentimeter nackter Haut preiszugeben. Es gibt nur wenige Stellen, an denen Dein – ebenfalls geschminkter – Hals sichtbar wird. Aber ansonsten ist Dein Körper vollständig bedeckt – Du trägst Perücken, Halskrausen, lange oder übergroße Filzhandschuhe, wodurch den Bildoberflächen der Anstrich eines Stoffbildes verliehen wird.

Sherman: Es gibt allerdings einige frühe Clownbilder, in denen meine Hände zu sehen sind. Ich habe sie am Anfang mit Make-up bedeckt, bis ich irgendwo las, daß Clowns immer Handschuhe tragen.

Graw: Auch wenn Du es bist, die die Darstellung der Clowns auf sich nimmt, zeigst Du nichts und exponierst Dich nicht selbst. Die Tendenz zu diesem Entzug hat es zwar schon in früheren Arbeiten gegeben, mir kam es jedoch so vor, als würdest Du ihn in den neuen Arbeiten zuspitzen.

Sherman: Nein, das hatte mehr mit der Tradition der Clowns selbst zu tun. Auch in früheren Arbeiten, zum Beispiel bei den Portraits von Frauen, die ich im Jahr 2000 gemacht habe, habe ich immer Make-up benutzt, wenn meine Arme oder andere Hautpartien zu sehen waren. Ich wollte das Make-up in meinem Gesicht komplettieren, um alles nahtlos erscheinen zu lassen. Die Haut meiner Arme sollte mit der des Gesichts übereinstimmen.

Graw: Mein Eindruck, daß das Thema Clown etwas mit dem Wunsch, sich vollständig unsichtbar zu machen, zu tun hat, ist also falsch?

Sherman: So habe ich darüber nicht nachgedacht. Was mich zu den Clowns hingezogen hat, war vielmehr die Möglichkeit, mich in verschiedene Clown-Persönlichkeiten hineinzuversetzen, was mir Vielschichtigkeit erlaubte: das Potential, traurig zu sein, gestört, ein Psychokiller... Mich interessierte das, was ich mir zu der als Clown geschminkten Person vorstelle. Was bringt diese Person dazu, ein Clown sein zu wollen? Wahrscheinlich ist es in den meisten Fällen die genuine Freude darüber, Leute zum Lachen zu bringen. Mich haben jedoch die Clowntypen mehr interessiert, bei denen es mir so vorkam, als gäbe es in ihrer Persönlichkeit etwas Schräges, Gestörtes.

Graw: Der Blick dieser Clowns ist durchgehend trübe und leer. Stumpfe, leere, ausdruckslose Augen, die nirgendwo hinzublicken scheinen. Es gibt keinen Adressaten mehr, der von ihnen angeblickt würde. Auch in den Bildern mit mehreren Clownfiguren wird kein Verhältnis zum Betrachter gesucht.

Sherman: Das mag an der Struktur der Bilder liegen: Ich hatte für sie Zirkusplakate im Kopf. Die Bilder sollten so aussehen, als hätte man sie einfach nur aus einem Werbeposter des Zirkus ausgeschnitten, in dem auf steife, künstliche Weise posiert wird, um die Idee des lustigen Clowns zu verkaufen – obwohl Clowns ja alles andere als lustig sind.

Graw: Die digital produzierten Hintergründe in Neonfarben sehen aus wie psychedelische Tapeten oder Op Art-Muster. Hier wird kein Raum suggeriert, sondern eine flächige, graphische Oberfläche. Wie kam es zu der Entscheidung für diese Hintergründe?

Sherman: Es hat Spaß gemacht, sie herzustellen, war aber auch viel Arbeit. Ich habe mit meinem Computer und Photoshop digital experimentiert. Das kam einer Herausforderung gleich, weil ich zunächst nicht realisierte, wieviel Arbeitsaufwand dies bedeuten würde. Als ich zunächst einmal eine allgemeine Idee für die Hintergründe entwickelt hatte, arbeitete ich gemeinsam mit einem Techniker an einem viel größeren Computer. Dann wurden die Übergänge fließender gestaltet oder die Haare erst durch den Hintergrund glaubwürdig gemacht.

Graw: Und Du selbst hast die Farben – Neonfarben – ausgewählt, die ja im übrigen mit der „day glow"-Mode dieser Saison (Sommer 2004) korrespondieren?

Sherman: Ja – ich habe einfach experimentiert. An Mode oder psychedelische Ästhetik habe ich allerdings nicht gedacht. Ich fragte mich vielmehr, was clownsmäßig aussehen und eine Anmutung von „funhouse" haben würde. Es gibt einen Hintergrund, für den ich die Nahaufnahme eines Balls, und einen anderen, für den ich Streifen mit grellen Farben verwendet habe. Das gefiel mir, weil es plötzlich so aussah, als ob sich der Hintergrund hinter den Clowns drehen würde. Meine Methode war eine des Ausprobierens.

Graw. War es das erste Mal, daß Du mit digitaler Bildproduktion experimentiert hast?

Sherman: Nein, vor ungefähr zwei Jahren habe ich ähnliche, allerdings viel einfachere Hintergründe gemacht. Und zwar für zwei Bilder – eines bezeichne ich als Typus „Gärtnerin" mit Strohhut vor orangefarbenem Hintergrund. Sie trägt Gärtnerhandschuhe. Eine andere nenne ich „Bimbo" – sie hat langes, blondes, gelocktes Haar und trägt dieses sehr häßliche, blaue Disco-Kleid und sieht so aus, als würde sie gleich „Hi" sagen [Sherman schlägt für die Imitation dieses „Hi" einen sehr hohen Tonfall an]. *Ich fand, daß die Figuren sehr gut funktionieren, daß der ursprüngliche weiße Hintergrund aber langweilig und trist aussah. Also fing ich an, auf meinem alten Laptop-Computer zu experimentieren, um herauszufinden, wie es aussehen würde, wenn die Hintergründe mit verschiedenen Farben überschwemmt werden.*

Graw: In Deiner Beschreibung der von Dir dargestellten Typen wird deutlich, wie viel Du über sie weißt, wie genau Du ihren Habitus studierst. Suchst Du Dir einen bestimmten Typus aus, den Du dann sozusagen selbst ausfüllst? Wie kommt es dazu, daß Du beschließt, eine bestimmte Person nicht nur zu spielen, sondern in sie hineinzuschlüpfen und sie auf bestimmte Weise ästhetisch auszugestalten?

Sherman: Manchmal entwickelt es sich linear und organisch. Bei der „Gärtnerin" fing es z.B. mit einer weißen Bauernbluse an, in die ich falsche Brüste hineingenäht hatte, was den Vorteil hatte, daß ich keine falschen Brüste an mir selbst befestigen mußte, sondern einfach nur in diese Bluse hineinschlüpfen konnte. Zuerst war sie ein völlig anderer Typ, hatte schwarze Haare und sah ein wenig wie eine italienische Mama aus. Ich habe diese Figur etwa fünf Mal photographiert und immer etwas hinzugefügt, zum Beispiel den Strohhut. Wenn etwas nicht funktionierte, photographierte ich sie wieder – etwa in Jeans.

Graw: Hattest Du ein bestimmtes Bild im Kopf, das Du erreichen wolltest, oder war dieser Prozeß im Ergebnis offen?

Sherman: Ich habe niemals etwas im Kopf, bevor ich den Film entwickelt und die Ergebnisse gesehen habe. Dann denke ich zum Beispiel: Hm, das, was ich ursprünglich machen wollte, hat offenbar nicht funktioniert. Aber hier ist etwas, was mich interessiert, vielleicht sollte ich versuchen, in diese Richtung weiterzugehen. Dann schlage ich eine neue Richtung ein, experimentiere, und etwas anderes, Unvorhergesehenes erregt mein Interesse.

Graw: Du beginnst mit einer bestimmten Versuchsanordnung und weißt nicht, was dabei herauskommen wird. Dann setzt Du Dich selbst dem Prozeß des Redigierens aus – wie eine Moderedakteurin, die sich selbst editiert.

Sherman: Genau.

Graw: Welches Verhältnis hast Du zu den Gesichtsausdrücken, die Du einnimmst? Ich denke, daß man eine Mimik nur dann überzeugend vorführen kann, wenn man sie mimetisch in sich aufgenommen hat, sich bis zu einem gewissen Grad mit ihr identifiziert.

Sherman: Auf jeden Fall. Es geht auch insofern um mich, als ich es ja bin, die diese Figuren darstellt. Ich kann nur so bescheuert oder schrecklich handeln wie meine Charaktere und denke, daß wir uns wahrscheinlich alle mit Teilen von ihnen identifizieren können. Was ich mache, ist Schauspielerei – ich trete zum Beispiel nicht in eine Figur ein und stelle mir vor, wie ihr Leben verlaufen ist oder wo sie lebt oder was für eine Familie sie hat. So weit begebe ich mich nicht hinein. Für mich ist viel entscheidender, was ich im Spiegel sehe – ich versuche das, was ich im Spiegel sehe, in etwas zu verwandeln, das für mich neu und überraschend ist.

Graw: Du sitzt vor dem Spiegel, und etwas Unerwartetes kommt vom Spiegel ausgehend auf Dich zu, dem Du gerecht werden mußt. Könnte man demzufolge sagen, daß das Publikum in erster Linie Du selbst bist? Vor allem bei den Arbeiten, in denen Du unterschiedliche Figuren montiert hast, scheinen die Clowns damit beschäftigt zu sein, sich selbst zuzusehen – auch wenn sie aus dem Bild heraustreten, grinsen sie sich selbst an. Dies erinnert mich an eine Deiner frühen Collagen – *The Press Interviews the Director as the Actress Poses from the Murder Mystery Series* (1976) –, in der Du die unterschiedlichen Akteure eines fiktiven Kriminalfalls spielst, zugleich Schauspielerin und Regisseur bist und Dir bei all diesen Rollen zuzusehen scheinst. Der Betrachter ist aus diesem Geschehen ausgeschlossen und verbannt.

Sherman: Tatsächlich versuche ich in erster Linie, mich selbst zu unterhalten. Wenn ich arbeite, soll es Spaß machen – Spaß nicht nur während der Arbeit, sondern auch danach. Ich will diejenige sein, der die Resultate gefallen, und an diesem Punkt ist es mir gleichgültig, ob es dem Betrachter gefällt oder nicht.

Graw: Mich interessiert auch das regressive Vokabular Deiner Clown-Bilder, da es meines Erachtens dem Spielerisch-Offenen Deines Verfahrens entspricht. Mal wird ein Strampelanzug getragen, mal ein Teddy gehalten oder ein Topf geschlagen. Man könnte dieses infantile Repertoire als Hinweis auf den grundsätzlich regressiven Zug Deiner Arbeitsweise lesen.

Sherman: Die Entscheidung für Spielzeug hatte eher damit zu tun, daß Clowns häufig Kinder unterhalten. Deshalb gibt es seltsame Dinge in den Bildern, etwa das Tier aus Luftballons. Einem Kind würde man dieses Objekt zeigen und sagen: Guck mal, dieses lustige kleine Ding. Viele Spielzeuge und Requisiten, die von Clowns benutzt werden, sind derart albern und klein.

Graw: Die Diptychon-Arbeit, die Du in Deiner Ausstellung der Galerie Metro Pictures (8. Mai–26. Juni) gezeigt hast, hat mir eben aufgrund dieses Luftballon-Hunds, den die eine Figur in der Hand hält, und aufgrund der am Hut befestigten Luftballon-Blumen der anderen Figur am besten gefallen. Der Hund ist für mich eindeutig eine Hommage an den *Balloon Dog* von Jeff Koons, von dem er sozusagen die Low Tech-Version darstellt.

Sherman: Der kleine Hund soll tatsächlich eine Anspielung auf diese Arbeit von Koons sein, die mir gut gefällt.

Graw: Dieses Objekt wird von der Clownfigur wie ein wertvolles oder antikes Stück mit spitzen Fingern vorgeführt.

Sherman: So als würde die Figur sagen: Dies ist mein kleines Hündchen.

Graw: In dem von Thames & Hudson publizierten Katalog über Deine Arbeit finden sich Pläne und Skizen, die zeigen, daß Du bei Deinen Projekten systematisch vorgehst. Zugleich werden, wie wir ja gesehen haben, Zufälle und Unvorhersehbarkeiten produktiv genutzt. Kannst Du dieses Verhältnis zwischen Konstruktion und Zufall genauer beschreiben?

Sherman: Ich versuche, alles geschehen zu lassen, und es gefällt mir, wenn die Dinge ganz zufällig geschehen. Deshalb ist es für mich immer einfacher, auf mich selbst zurückzugreifen. Denn wenn ich mit Puppen oder Schaufensterpuppen arbeite, muß ich alles im voraus planen. Alles muß für den Moment, wo ich photographiere, vorbereitet sein, nichts darf dem Zufall überlassen bleiben. Für eine dieser Serien habe ich dennoch den Zufallsfaktor eingesetzt, indem ich unterschiedliche Filme benutzte. Ich habe entweder mit Diafilm photographiert und den Abzug in verschiedenen Chemikalien entwickelt oder einen „Printfilm" genommen, den ich dann als Dia entwickelte. Je nach Film und Entwicklungsmethode, änderten sich die Farben komplett. Das sind die Methoden, mit denen ich diesen „Stilleben" den Zufall aufzuzwingen versuche. Die eine Hälfte des Diptychon-Bildes verdankt sich im übrigen einem Zufall. Als ich das Photo machte, mußte ich blinzeln. Nur funktionierten die anderen Versionen mit geöffneten Augen für mich nicht. So wichtig es mir ist, den Zufall zu seinem Recht kommen zu lassen, bedarf jede Arbeit doch auch der Strukturierung. Sobald ich ein paar Dinge photographiert habe, fange ich an, sie zu analysieren. Handelt es sich z.B. um Ganzkörperaufnahmen, dann frage ich mich, ob ich vielleicht ein paar Close-ups brauche. Ich mag es, wenn sich die Dinge mischen, wenn sich alles voneinander unterscheidet. Deshalb mache ich solche Listen und Pläne.

Graw: Du arbeitest ja auch in Serien – und jede Serie schränkt Möglichkeiten ein und basiert auf einer inhaltlichen Prämisse. Wie kommt es zu diesen Vorgaben?

Sherman: Als ich im Jahr 2000 die Gruppe von Frauen machte, die ich „Hollywood-Typen" nenne, hatte ich folgende Erklärung für diese Serie: Es sollten Photos von Leuten sein, die sich als Schauspieler anpreisen, aber in Wahrheit als Sekretärin, Hausfrau oder Gärtner arbeiten. Die Idee war, daß diese Leute sich mit aller Kraft zu verkaufen suchen und dem Betrachter die Frage stellen: Wollen Sie mich nicht einstellen? Zwei Jahre, nachdem ich diese Serie gemacht hatte, wollte ich weiter daran arbeiten. Das war 2002, unmittelbar nach dem 11. September. Ich photographierte andere Typen, noch mehr Frauen, hatte aber keine Idee von der Richtung, die die Sache nehmen sollte. Es fehlte die Strukturierung. Ich beendete diese Gruppe von Arbeiten und quälte mich eine Weile mit der Frage, was zu tun sei.

Graw: Und wie fanden sich dann die Clowns ein?

Sherman: Wenn ich versuche, mich zu inspirieren, räume ich gewöhnlich mein Atelier auf und gehe Schubladen durch. Es gibt so viele Dinge, die ich aufbewahrt habe – Props, Kostüme und

Perücken. Ich wühle also ein bißchen herum und schaue, ob mich etwas anspricht. Dabei bin ich auf einen alten Schlafanzug gestoßen, den ich auf dem Flohmarkt gekauft hatte. Er war sehr alt und fiel auseinander, aber jemand hatte ihn in ein Clownskostüm verwandelt. Zwar habe ich ihn bis heute nicht verwendet, aber ich dachte, daß dies doch vielleicht eine großartige Sache sei, die sich verfolgen ließe. Und dann fiel mir auf, daß es ja derart viele Typen von Clowns gibt, daß sich praktisch alles benutzen läßt, angefangen von irgendeinem Lumpen bis hin zu Kleiderkombinationen. Es gibt ja auch Clowns, die einfach nur Jeans und ein grellfarbenes T-Shirt anhaben. Nur weil sie eine Perücke und weiße Schminke tragen, sind sie ein Clown. Ich hatte also den Eindruck, hier auf fruchtbares Terrain gestoßen zu sein.

Graw: Wenn Du vor dem Spiegel mit unterschiedlichen Kostümen, Haltungen und Gesichtsausdrücken experimentierst, bist Du dann alleine oder halten sich Assistenten in Deiner Nähe auf?

Sherman: Ich bin allein.

Graw: Du bist allein im Studio – auch ein modernistisches Thema. Statt dem Bild vom Künstler als Unternehmer oder Firmenleiter zu entsprechen, weist Deine Arbeitsweise in eine andere Richtung. Das Bild des einsam in seinem Atelier arbeitenden Künstlers wird aktiviert, der prozeßhaft arbeitet, sich Zufallsfunden überläßt und die relative Autonomie dieses Ortes produktiv zu nutzen weiß.

Sherman: Wahrscheinlich. Ich gehe so vor, weil ich so am besten arbeiten kann. Als ich einmal versucht habe, mich mit anderen Leuten zu umgeben – nur als Experiment –, hat es nicht wirklich funktioniert. Ich benehme mich dann sehr gespreizt und habe das Gefühl, mich zurückhalten zu müssen. Außerdem treibe ich andere Leute nicht so an, wie ich mich selbst antreibe. Mir kommt es so vor, als würde ich ihre Zeit stehlen – auch dann noch, wenn ich sie bezahle, möchte ich, daß alles glatt läuft, damit sie auch Spaß haben.

Graw: Vielleicht ließe sich die Situation mit der vergleichen, wo man sich selbst im Spiegel betrachtet und ein anderer einem dabei zusieht. Das ist immer unangenehm, so als würde man bei einem intimen Selbstbezug ertappt. Der Gesichtsausdruck, den man vor dem Spiegel einnimmt, ist ja nicht unbedingt für die Öffentlichkeit bestimmt, auch wenn man vielleicht eine Pose probt, mit der man sich später zeigt.

Sherman: Es fällt mir außerdem schwer, Leuten vorzuschreiben, was sie zu tun haben. Das hat wahrscheinlich damit zu tun, daß ich nicht unbedingt ein Kontrollfreak bin und intuitiv weiß, was ich will. Nur – da diese Intuition die meine ist, werde auch nur ich wissen oder sehen, ob etwas funktioniert.

Graw: Dieses Wissen läßt sich nicht weitergeben oder delegieren, auch wenn es natürlich Kriterien dafür gibt, die allerdings schwer vermittelbar sind. Auch Pollock konnte ja seinen Dripping-Prozeß nicht abgeben.

Sherman: [lacht] *Ja – er konnte niemand anderem erklären, wie man die Farbe auf das Bild werfen muß.*

Graw: Im Vergleich zu Deinen frühen *Film Stills* hat die Bedeutung von Situationen heute abgenommen. An die Stelle räumlicher Situationen oder Interieurs sind eher abstrakte Hintergründe getreten. Ich habe mich gefragt, warum Du die Figuren nicht mehr in ein Milieu plazierst. Könnte es sein, daß Dich Situationen und Szenarien heute weniger interessieren als psychische Befindlichkeiten?

Sherman: Am deutlichsten sieht man diesen Unterschied an den Film Stills, *für die ich Hintergründe benutzt habe, die wirklich existierten. Hier zum Beispiel* [zeigt auf das Bild *Untitled Film Still* # 43, 1979] *ist der Hintergrund nicht fingiert, ich saß wirklich da, auf diesem Baum. Auch bei einigen der Interieur-Aufnahmen handelt es sich um Räumlichkeiten, an denen ich selbst gelebt habe. Nur daß ich die Möbel so umarrangierte, daß es aussah wie das Bühnenbild einer Wohnung. Solche Hintergründe sind mir in letzter Zeit nicht mehr so wichtig gewesen – jedenfalls gilt das für die Serie der Frauen aus dem Jahr 2000. Und bei den Clowns wollte ich den inneren Eindruck vermitteln, daß sie sich in deinem oder ihrem eigenen Kopf befinden.*

Graw: Es geht um mentale Räume, die dargestellt werden sollen?

Sherman: Ja. Waren die Film Stills *noch narrativ strukturiert in dem Sinne, als es ein Szenario gab, interessieren mich narrative Strukuren heute weniger. Ich habe zwar darüber nachgedacht, noch einmal so vorzugehen, nur möchte ich natürlich vermeiden, daß diese neuen Arbeiten dann wie die* Film Stills *aussehen. Augenblicklich interessiert es mich mehr, in einem Kopf-Raum oder in psychische Räume einzutreten, so als würde ich malen und die Dinge einfach erfinden. Nichts muß Sinn machen, man kann Dinge zusammenwerfen, weil sie einfach gut zusammen aussehen.*

kestnergesellschaft
Goseriede 11
30159 Hannover
Germany
Fon +49 511 70120 0
Fax +49 511 70120 20
kestner@kestner.org
www.kestner.org

Catalog to accompany the exhibition | Katalog anläßlich der Ausstellung
Cindy Sherman
kestnergesellschaft Hannover
24. September – 7. November 2004

Edited by | Herausgegeben von
Veit Görner and | Maik Schlüter, kestnergesellschaft, Hannover

Translations into English | Übersetzungen ins Englische
Jeremy Gaines (foreword and essay), Brian Currid (interview)

Design: Cindy Sherman and The Grenfell Press, New York
Lithography, printing and binding: EBS, Verona

ISBN 978-3-8296-0168-9

A Schirmer/Mosel Production
www.schirmer-mosel.com